Praise for *Pilgrims in the Kingdom*

"We go to God not by walking but by loving," said Augustine. His fear was that pilgrims too often turn into tourists. This delightful book proves that pilgrimage can be a way of loving. Joining castles and cathedrals, caves and islands, Catholic and Protestant places, it combines the arts of the travel writer, the church historian, and the interpreter of sacred texts. All of this echoes through the antiphonal voices of a man and woman who love (and evoke love for) the God they meet in the exquisite places they describe.

—BELDEN C. LANE
Professor of Theological Studies
Saint Louis University

David and Deborah's essays demonstrate that true pilgrimage occurs in both our inner and our outer lives. This book is an elegant guide to both journeys. The Douglases provide a guide to popular, proven pilgrimage sites, as well as encouragement to seek out one's private heroes.

—DONNA OSTHAUS
Pilgrimage Leader in the United Kingdom,
France, and Italy

This book is wonderfully evocative as well as quite useful. As you read the descriptions of each holy place, you feel you are there with the authors in their journey of pilgrimage and discovery. They infectiously convey their own joy and excitement at what they find. Their sensitive evocation of spiritual experience is matched by sound, practical advice on accessing the places covered in this book. I commend *Pilgrims in the Kingdom* to all who want to know more about Britain's sacred sites and special places and who wish to explore them either on foot or from their own armchairs.

—REV. DR. IAN BRADLEY
Reader in Practical Theology and Church History
University of St. Andrews

Whether read at home or on the road, *Pilgrims in the Kingdom* is a guide to the great souls of Christian Britain and the places they inhabited. In their meditations on the intermingling of lives and places, Deborah and David Douglas begin with the mystery of the Incarnation—that holiness arises in time and space, leaving behind traces for those who seek to find it.

—DANA GREENE
Author of *Evelyn Underhill: Artist of the In* ...
Dean and CEO, Oxford C ...

Deborah and David Douglas are witnesses. They give us a firsthand account of places where God transformed the minds and hearts of women and men who in turn transformed the world. To read this work is to be on a holy pilgrimage, one that widens our horizons and expands our hearts.

—ROBERT F. MORNEAU
Auxiliary Bishop of Green Bay

In this outstanding collection of personal travelers' tales, David and Deborah Douglas, writing both as our guides and our companions, invite us to participate in a journey inspired by people and place. This is a generous, openhearted book in which anticipation, experience, and reflection are skillfully woven and shared. Written in a style that is fresh and stimulating, here is an informative yet searching pilgrims' guide. Those encouraged to join the authors as they discover and explore Celtic, medieval, and modern saints and sites will find themselves drawn to a deeper understanding of the place of divine encounter in their own lives.

—REV. LINDSAY SPENDLOVE
Director, Green Blade Retreat Centre, Suffolk, England
Former chaplain to the Chelmsford Diocesan House of Retreat, Pleshey

We live at a time when people are increasingly fascinated by spiritual pilgrimage and what is nowadays known in the tourist world as transformational travel. In this context, *Pilgrims in the Kingdom* will surely find a ready audience and a warm welcome. Based on their extended and intense experience of living and traveling in the United Kingdom, Deborah and David Douglas have gathered together a very personal and attractive selection of their favorite Christian spiritual sites in Britain. This includes an appendix of helpful Travel Notes. The ecumenical breadth and spirit of inclusivity should entice a wide range of readers.

Writing in turn, Deborah and David introduce the reader to different locations with a mixture of physical descriptions, personal anecdote, history, quotation, and thoughtful reflections. Through the medium of their own pilgrimage, Deborah and David remind us yet again of the extraordinary power of a sense of place to shape our religious imaginations and to feed our spiritual quest.

—PHILIP SHELDRAKE
William Leech Professor, University of Durham, England

PILGRIMS
in the
KINGDOM

Travels in Christian Britain

Deborah Douglas and David Douglas

Photographs by Joan Myers

for Joan & Hoyt, fellow pilgrims, friends in God, Deborah + David  *Vayan con Dios —*

Deborah Douglas, *David S Douglas*

▼ UPPER
ROOM BOOKS®
NASHVILLE

An extension of the copyright page is on page 245.

Cover design: Gore Studio, Inc. / www.GoreStudio.com
Cover and interior photographs: Joan Myers / www.joanmyers.com
Map by Deborah Reade
First printing: 2004

Library of Congress Cataloging-in-Publication Data
Douglas, Deborah Smith.
Pilgrims in the kingdom : travels in Christian Britain / Deborah Douglas and David Douglas.
    p. cm.
Includes bibliographical references and index.
ISBN 0-8358-9872-5
1. Great Britain—Guidebooks. 2. Christian pilgrims and pilgrimages—Great Britain—Guidebooks.
3. Christian antiquities—Great Britain—Guidebooks. 4. Christian shrines—Great Britain—Guidebooks.
I. Douglas, David, 1949– II. Title.
DA650.D68 2004
263'.04241—dc22
                                                                    2003022891

Printed in the United States of America

Contents

〰

For Katie and Emily

Acknowledgments

A WHOLE HOST of generous fellow travelers has companioned, encouraged, and directed us on the long journey of this book's creation.

From the beginning, Nancy Arnon Agnew, Richard Holland, Annie Piper, and Cindy Quicksall Landsberg have been, as ever in our writing lives, invaluable first readers, editors, and friends. Rebecca Laird, Belden Lane, John Mogabgab, Robert Morneau, and Ian Bradley gave us wise advice and encouragement at crucial times. Philip Sheldrake pored over those first maps with us and introduced us to St. Beuno's. We owe a great deal to Sister Mary Joaquin Bitler for her luminous presence in our lives and her love and prayers.

We are grateful to Michael Tobert in St. Andrews, Jacquie and Andrew Kerr at Whithorn, and Cathleen and Dennis Archer at Little Gidding for generous hospitality and many kindnesses. Our thanks as well to Marjory Farmer and other members of the staff at the St. Andrews University Library. Joan Myers's photographs have enriched our own view of these places; we are grateful to Joan and her husband, Bernie Lopez, for sharing our delight in the journey.

We are indebted to JoAnn Miller, Anne Trudel, Sarah Schaller-Linn, and Denise Duke at Upper Room Books for encouragement in shepherding the manuscript into print.

Ann and Dick Rowe, Miriam and Will Overholt, Susie and Fred Harburg, Becky Donohue, Jane Gee, Kyra Kerr, Chris Johnson, and Bud Redding have upheld us all along the way with their enthusiasm, prayers, and friendship.

Finally, we are uniquely grateful to our daughters, Katie and Emily, both excellent traveling companions who grew up along with this book.

Pilgrims
in the Kingdom

ATLANTIC OCEAN

NORTH SEA

IRISH SEA

SCOTLAND

ENGLAND

WALES

0   50   100   150 kilometers

0   50   100 miles

IONA •
(St. Columba)

ST. ANDREWS •

EDINBURGH •
(St. Margaret)

LINDISFARNE •
(HOLY ISLAND)
(St. Aidan & St. Cuthbert)

WHITHORN •
(St. Ninian)

PENDLE HILL •
(George Fox)

YORK •
(Mary Ward &
Margaret Clitherow)

NORWICH •
(Julian of Norwich)

ST. BEUNO'S •
(Gerard Manley Hopkins)

LITTLE GIDDING •
(Nicholas Ferrar
& T.S. Eliot)

COVENTRY CATHEDRAL •

OLNEY •
(John Newton)

PLESHEY •
(Evelyn Underhill)

OXFORD •
(C.S. Lewis)

LONDON •
ALDERSGATE ST.
(John Wesley)

BEMERTON •
(George Herbert)

CANTERBURY
CATHEDRAL

N
W   E
S

Reade

Introduction

⁓

$\mathcal{T}$HE JOURNEY BEGAN for us with the names of places in England, Scotland, and Wales. Some sites were well-known, the destinations of ancient pilgrimage trails. Others were seldom visited, unmarked on all but the most tenacious maps. Long identified with men and women who had lived their faith boldly, each place had mediated the Christian story over the centuries, often drawing travelers closer to God.

With the prospect of a sabbatical year away from our work in the United States, we pored over a map of the United Kingdom, pencils in hand, as a tentative itinerary came into view. Britain provided a breadth of Christian landscape perhaps unsurpassed in the world, with sites steeped in Celtic, Catholic, and Protestant traditions. Beckoning us were chapels and sea caves, mountains and cathedrals, retreat centers and holy islands. Could sojourning in these places, listening more attentively to the lives of people linked to these sites, help us understand their experiences of God and, more to the point, bring us closer to God as well?

We had long known of Iona, for example, off the west coast of Scotland, where Saint Columba founded a monastery that illumined much of northern Britain. But what would it be like to walk the island? How did you get to it, and where would you stay? Why does the Celtic saint's legacy attract people even today? "To tell the story of Iona," one writer noted invitingly, "is to go back to God and to end in God."[1]

Methodist friends had often alluded to John Wesley's Aldersgate Street experience. In some ways Methodism traces its history to this corner of London where Wesley had felt his heart "strangely warmed," overwhelmed with an assurance that his sins were forgiven.[2] Could we return to Aldersgate, not to recreate Wesley's experience—as though epiphanies could be snatched like butterflies—but rather to glimpse his understanding of God's forgiveness, that it might shed light on our own?

The ancient city of Norwich harbored a memory of Lady Julian, the fourteenth-century mystic who wrote zealously of God's love and provided spiritual advice from her solitary cell. By immersing ourselves in Julian's writings and prayerfully returning to sites associated with her, could we ourselves sense more fully God's imperishable love?

Britain offered this spectrum of Christian sites from the fourth century to the twenty-first all within a nation smaller in size than our home state of New Mexico. From Coventry Cathedral to Saint Margaret's tiny stone chapel at the heart of Edinburgh Castle, from C. S. Lewis's Oxford to T. S. Eliot's Little Gidding, from the pastoral Wales of Gerard Manley Hopkins's poetry to the English market town of Olney where John Newton penned "Amazing Grace"—all across the United Kingdom were places where men and women had borne generous witness to the faith within them. What attracted us to a location was not so much its physical topography as its spiritual biography.

Reassuring his disciples in Jerusalem's upper room, Jesus promised that the Holy Spirit would "bring to your remembrance all that I have said to you" (John 14:26, RSV). We traveled in the light of that promise, asking ourselves: "What is here, in this place specifically, that the Holy Spirit might bring to our remembrance? If we will but listen, what aspect of the will and love of God is evinced by this place and by the persons who lived and sought God here?"

In our experience, the places in this book have been far more than sites of historical interest. They have, in different ways, been settings where that sort of holy listening, that kind of Spirit-led remembering, has happened to us. We found ourselves repeatedly recalling T. S. Eliot's verse from "Little Gidding" (not least at Little Gidding itself):

You are not here to verify,
Instruct yourself, or inform curiosity
Or carry report. You are here to kneel
Where prayer has been valid.[3]

We set out to visit these sites from St. Andrews, Scotland. We chose this town that feels like a village as our base for several reasons. Though unaffiliated with its medieval university, we found that St. Andrews provided us with a priceless library collection on British Christianity, a girls' school for our two daughters, and, not least, a home beside the North Sea. To the amazement of our neighbors, we even relished Scotland's rain, which fell like a blessing on parched New Mexicans.

A pattern emerged during what became two years of residence in Scotland, and during subsequent, shorter returns: After a period of preparation, having distilled all we could from the university's library, we left St. Andrews, often from the nearest train station at the village of Leuchars, our trips timed as much as possible to good weather, thin crowds, and favorable tides.

We usually ventured out singly in our travel rather than in tandem. With our daughters in school, one parent needed to remain in St. Andrews. We also preferred to write in our own voices rather than settle for negotiated phrases. In addition, many of the destinations offered contemplative opportunities for silence and reflection, often best appreciated in solitude. Though most names on our list of places and people long had influenced us both, we gradually sorted out respective itineraries, each yielding to the other's deeper affinity.

Kneeling in these places "where prayer has been valid" has deepened the way we pray everywhere. We have come to see, with Elizabeth Barrett Browning, that "Earth's crammed with heaven, and every common bush afire with God."[4] As Gerard Manley Hopkins perceived, "The world is charged with the grandeur of God."[5]

Of those places we chose to chronicle—settings illustrative of Britain's vast spiritual landscape—many seemed to illumine certain facets of faith in particular. Scotland's Whithorn, for example, where Saint Ninian carried the gospel to unruly Picts, revealed the burden of witness and a call for Christians to speak despite unfavorable circumstances. Canterbury Cathedral, with its East Chapel's focus on contemporary Christian martyrdom, put into relief the cost of discipleship from Thomas Becket down to the current day. Where better to wrestle with difficulties of forgiveness in our own lives than in the bombed-out ruins of old Coventry Cathedral and amid Coventry's new, postwar Cathedral's dedication to reconciliation?

We hesitate to call these destinations "sacred sites," as though some settings (and by implication not others) offer domains of the holy. Perhaps, as Thomas More suggested, "there are places where God seems to want to be worshipped"; indeed, rocky outcrops of beauty like Lindisfarne and Iona can direct attention toward heaven just as observatories turn eyes to the sky. But at times pilgrims give credit to extraordinary place for experiences wrought more by dedication of ordinary time. After she heard visitors refer to Iona as a "thin place" where "there's very little between Iona and the Lord," Evelyn Underhill remarked, "I am far from denying that from our human point of view, some places are a great deal thinner than others: but to the eyes of worship, the whole of the visible world, even its most unlikely patches, is rather thin."[6]

This is one reason we include places off well-worn pilgrim tracks. As the poet William Cowper, coauthor with John Newton of *Olney Hymns,* wrote from England's market town of Olney:

> Jesus, where'er thy people meet,
> There they behold thy mercy-seat;
> Where'er they seek thee thou art found,
> And ev'ry place is hallow'd ground.[7]

Our journey has yielded a wide view of the church in the world and a clearer perspective of our own calling. We discovered that we had not so much taken the journey as allowed it to take us—and strengthen and challenge us, and send us at times by unforeseen routes. As George Macdonald once said of stories, true journeys somehow don't seem to end. "The path of life is not only in eternity but toward eternity," notes Grace Adolphsen Brame, "and the journey is not finished."[8]

For those who would visit these sites, either alone or in groups, we provide practical travel information in the Travel Notes. "The idea of pilgrimage is one that we badly need to recover today," urges British writer Ian Bradley.[9] Down through the centuries, the hope of drawing closer to God frequently provided the primary motivation for a journey.

Particularly for visitors to Britain descended from Celtic, Catholic, and Reformed traditions, pilgrimage remains a way of travel that can orient lives of faith.

We intend these chapters no less for armchair travelers; insight comes not only in transit along Damascus roads but in quiet after leaving Emmaus roads. For readers unlikely to set out in person on British byways, the men and women chronicled here, via their letters and journals, essays and poems, remain companions for an interior passage of faith, reminding us that indeed "we are surrounded by so great a cloud of witnesses" (Heb. 12:1).

We have arranged the chapters in chronological order, according to the time period of the person most closely associated with the site. A journey that begins with the names of places leads to the brave, visionary, joyful people who lived there. Though C. S. Lewis, T. S. Eliot, John Wesley, and Julian of Norwich are hardly neglected, the faith experiences of some other men and women included in this book have languished in out-of-print passages. Exploring accounts of early Celtic saints, medieval martyrs, and the first Quakers can lead contemporary readers to wellsprings of courage and witness.

We hope these chapters will be useful to others as background on the landscape of Christian Britain, as a guide to plan a route of one's own, and as a reflective aid to prayer. Our great hope, of course, like John Bunyan's in *The Pilgrim's Progress,* is that "this book will make a traveller of thee"—if not to the places cited in these pages, then to wherever in your life God is waiting to be found.

St. Ninian's Cave, Whithorn

Chapter 1

Whithorn and Saint Ninian

"The cradle of Scottish Christianity"

The journey began here for us, along the southwest coast of Scotland on the Galloway peninsula. If you can, seek out Ninian's sea cave in the quiet of the day.

—DAVID

I WALK TO THE CAVE in the early morning, down an archway of sycamore, ash, and oak, along an insistent stream and through a final cleft that frames the approaching sea. A right turn across a beach of smooth stones leads me up to the mouth of Saint Ninian's cave.

The shallow recess sits a few yards above sea level, a damp, narrow crevice in Silurian slate, twenty feet high and equally deep, cloistered from any gale that might batter this southwestern tip of Scotland.

Sixteen centuries ago, tradition tells us, Ninian (c. 360–c. 432) walked here for silence and prayer, briefly withdrawing from his monastic community three miles away at Whithorn. Before arriving at this coastal cell myself, I had imagined the Celtic saint huddled within the crevice's damp shadows like Saint Cuthbert in his Farne Island hut, purposely having dimmed daylight lest the sun's dazzle distract him.

But now I envision Ninian on fine early mornings outside his cave on a tier of stones, sea-watching, gull-glancing, and letting God speak in the rinsed morning.

Inside the cave I try to discern the rumored crosses etched into the slate. As my eyes grow sharper, I can see them slowly emerge from the darkness, faint as Ninian's story itself.

What little we know about Ninian comes from a handful of sources, chiefly a short, captivating biography written in the twelfth century by the Cistercian monk Aelred of Rievaulx and a few words by the chronicler Bede in the eighth century.

A hundred years before Columba arrived at Iona, Ninian founded in 397 the first monastic settlement in what is now Scotland. Built from local shales and slates and lime-plastered white to glisten like a lighthouse in the sun, the monastery took on the name *Candida Casa*—the Latin becoming Whithorn (White House) in its Anglo-Saxon rendering.

British-born and Roman-educated, Ninian preached and told the Christian story to the southern Picts, aboriginal inhabitants of Scotland. His father had ruled as a king of the Celtic tribe of Britons, but the son turned his back on royalty. Like Saint Francis sloughing off his wealth, Ninian exchanged entitlements for another currency. Not only compassion and zeal but also a certain breadth characterized his life; Ninian excluded no creature from God's grace, gathering even cattle and sheep together at night for a blessing. Biographers shower praise on him: devout, sagacious, bold, and, not least, attentive. An awareness of God graced Ninian like an astronomer's eye fixed to the sky. "It is characteristic of the saints," observed Lucy Menzies, "that they tend gradually, little by little, to be transformed by that which they seek."[1]

The word *first* colors each reference to Ninian and Whithorn: the first stone church, the first monastic settlement, the first missionary in Scotland to tell others the gospel story. History leaves unanswered the question of who first told Ninian himself.

⁓

At the end of rolling countryside dipping down to the sea, Whithorn lies near both England and Ireland. From this coastal foothold, away from the crossroads of wars, Ninian witnessed boldly throughout Galloway's peninsula. Celtic monks "alternated between periods of intense activity running their busy monastic *familia* and weeks or months of solitary withdrawal," writes Ian Bradley in *Colonies of Heaven*.[2]

The Celtic saint's light pierced a dark inland landscape, humbling the painted Picts and unknotting tribal wars, as Aidan also would do later from Lindisfarne. My family name comes originally from this Scottish region; perhaps an unruly ancestor encountered Ninian himself. One author claims that "Ninian rescued Picts from barbarism," turning them aside from idols, brutal ceremonies, and cycles of vengeance.[3]

Such achievement can trigger scoffing today. Skeptics ask, "Isn't 'barbarism' in the beholder's eye, and paganism merely a cultural preference?" Disputing the disease, they doubt a cure by the Cross. Moreover, they question Ninian's very effectiveness: the Picts (so named by Roman soldiers for painting their skin) may eventually have washed off their conversion like one of their pigments. Which brings us face-to-face with Robin Lane Fox's observation: The degree to which people ever became Christianized is a problem that recurs awkwardly in history "before foundering, as always, on the observable experience of our own lives."[4]

So perhaps Ninian retreated here to this cave in the wake of failure and exhaustion. Like a later Scottish missionary, David Livingstone (whose lifetime tally of African converts numbered two), Ninian took solace in the scriptural charge to disciples that skims over "be effective" to fasten on the mandate "be faithful."

Three sites in particular remain linked to Ninian: this damp, tapering cave of retreat; the monastic ruins of *Candida Casa* at Whithorn, three miles to the north; and lastly, down the coast, the Isle of Whithorn, where pilgrims once disembarked and knelt before walking inland to *Candida Casa*. These three equidistant landmarks—"a trio of localities which in historic importance and in sanctity are unsurpassed in the kingdom"[5]— introduced some visitors to the Trinity and offered down the centuries a destination of solitude, witness, and prayer.

The Isle of Whithorn, a slender finger of turf and stone, juts into the Solway Firth a few miles down this indented coastline. Ninian's legacy of healing miracles and posthumous relics attracted a steady train of medieval pilgrims, and after crossing the Irish Sea, they exchanged rolling ships for the isle's steadying hummocks. A thirteenth-century chapel, built atop an even older one, still deflects the wind and smooths the gait of anxious visitors.

A portion of the isle, joined now by causeway to the mainland, hums with the sound of harbor boats. But much of its ground retains an isolated charm, grooved with sheep trails running past rocky outcrops covered with lichen. At low tide, wet white stones gleam as if freshly painted, hinting that these have provided the building blocks for Ninian's settlement, stones so dazzling they disdained further lime-washed shine.

Like the tenacious coastal settings of Iona and Lindisfarne, *Candida Casa* served as a whitewashed monument, a lighthouse designed not to warn but to attract, signaling that here are shoals on which one would wish to run aground.

In nearby Whithorn, now a town of twelve hundred people, a mound barely higher than the surrounding countryside entombs the probable site of Ninian's ancient monastery. Above ground, the grassy rise hosts two churches—one new, the other ancient and roofless—along with wind-effaced tombstones and fenced archeological digs. The Whithorn Trust's highly regarded excavation work has burrowed through sixteen hundred years of history with Christian, Northumbrian, and Scandinavian layers of influence.

A controversy continues to swirl about the place. Does the mound with its persuasive ruins and artifacts indeed reveal the site of *Candida Casa,* or could Ninian's monastery actually lie buried on the Isle of Whithorn? Ancient descriptions and current historians take issue with one another, trying to pinpoint the original locale of "the cradle of Scottish Christianity."[6] The dispute mirrors the Holy Land's conflicts over terrain—whether Christ's temporary tomb could be traced to Jerusalem's Church of the Holy Sepulcher, despite the appeal of the tranquil, more evocative Garden Tomb.

Was the actual site here or only near here? Whithorn's feuds point up the limits of identifying precise ground as sacred space, as though we could pin down holiness in the crosshairs of archeology.

Ninian's monks at *Candida Casa* lived in individual cells while sharing at the same time a corporate life. "His form of settlement was unlike anything that had been seen in Britain before," explains Shirley Toulson in *Celtic Journeys,* "yet it was to become the model throughout the Dark Ages."[7]

The monks prayed and taught, studied and copied the Gospels and Psalms. Graced by "humility, compassion and devotion," the community drew students from Ireland and England.[8] On this promontory "the seeds of Celtic Christianity took root and grew to flavour not only Britain but the whole of western Europe."[9]

Peering into the ruins, contemporary visitors can imagine monks bent assiduously in prayer, like later saints who "did not try to escape from the world" but "tried rather to transform it."[10] At other fields across Britain, crowds stand musing, anguished by battles that sowed the land with tombstones. But Whithorn's grassy mound elicited a quieter sacrifice. On this field people gave lives rather than taking them. Pilgrims today can still unearth their shards of dedication.

⌒

I slept comfortably last night at a bed-and-breakfast named after Saint Ninian. The owners are kind-eyed, humorous, and accommodating. As we stood in their kitchen after breakfast, they showed me honey gathered from their bees, one jar of heather honey, the other drawn from sycamore, hawthorn, and bluebonnet.

In addition to running the bed-and-breakfast, the husband and wife serve as lay Missionaries of Charity, the first two such associates of Mother Teresa's order in all of Scotland. They have vowed poverty, obedience, conjugal chastity, and wholehearted and free service to the poorest of the poor. They earmark profits from the bed-and-breakfast for deprived families, convey medicines to the sick in Rumania, and take children in Whithorn on outings. Their compassion, quiet and deep, mingles with a certain gravity about God and lightness about themselves.

They mention a friend of theirs, a priest, who once observed that "we can lose a lifetime practice of prayer in two days." Why, we ask ourselves, should a devotional life so quickly atrophy? Why should God seem to slip out of sight? The answer, we agree, glints in our question: growing slack, we break our span of attention. Inattentive to our daily bread, we try to arrange for a weekly supply.

The medieval monk Aelred of Rievaulx, after extolling Saint Ninian's love and humility, once groused nostalgically from his window on the twelfth century: "When I consider the devout walk and conversation of this man, I am ashamed of our negligence; I am ashamed of the sloth of this miserable age."[11] Lest I too be inclined to view Ninian's characteristics as quaint relics, I see them reflected in faces across the kitchen.

The bed-and-breakfast sheltered only two other guests last night, a couple from Glasgow, she a tall, attractive woman in her late forties, and he a red-bearded sculptor with wild, unkempt hair. A raconteur with a deep bass voice, he put his heavy boots on the living room table after dinner, told work-related stories with gruff irreverence, then asked what brought me to Britain.

I told him that Deborah and I intended to visit such sites as Lindisfarne and Iona, and Canterbury and Coventry Cathedrals. I spoke of places linked to Julian of Norwich, George Fox, and Evelyn Underhill and mentioned qualities—a mysticism checked by accountability, an evangelism infused by compassion—that drew me to them. As I concluded, I watched the sculptor's piercing eyes and felt that he little understood my interest. This wooly-haired druid would have seemed more at home at Stonehenge than Canterbury Cathedral.

To my surprise, however, he began to speak about a trip he had made to Iona years before. "We took a wee boat down to the jetty," he recalled, looking away. "People were all a-flutter, chattering, feet moving fast, and then partway across the Sound, you can see the change. They're walking differently; they're being different. I don't know why. But it happened to us. People come looking for something."

The sculptor turned his attention back to Ninian and Whithorn as he rose to go to bed. "Tomorrow morning go early to Ninian's cave. Go before anyone else gets there."

And so I have, walking in the quiet to this place of retreat where people have returned to remember. On the night before his death, in one of his last utterances to his disciples, Jesus promised that the Holy Spirit will "bring to your remembrance all that I have said to you" (John 14:26, RSV). At times faith seems to have less to do with revelation than recollection. But where in our lives do we set out to remember? An old guidebook to Scotland described Iona as "the calling place" of pilgrims. With that double meaning—not only a place to call upon but a place to heed a call—these settings of retreat can orient us toward God and provide direction upon our return.

Far down the beach I glimpse two people emerging from the archway of trees. They appear in no hurry to reach the cave, and, sitting down on the stones to look out on the Solway Firth, they give me a few more minutes of solitude.

Here near the cave bracketed by slate cliffs, I see Ninian most clearly. He returned to drink in this restorative silence, no doubt arriving on wobbly legs and weariness in some years. In the sweet loneliness of the sea cave, Ninian's boldness, elsewhere ground away, could be salted beside the waves.

I have taken my place at the end of a sixteen-hundred-year line of visitors to this place. Why have I come? To touch these incised crosses? "To kneel where prayer has been valid"? To gather my own bearings on a journey toward, in Thomas à Kempis's words, "the country of everlasting clarity"?[12]

As I leave the cave I walk over the cobbled beach, selecting along the way a handful of granite stones as gifts. Innumerable, smooth, and glistening, they seem beautiful as pearls. I spend more time considering the choices than I would before a display case.

I intend to bypass the two visitors seated on the stones, leaving them in their silence, but from a hundred yards away I hear my name called out in greeting and recognize the other guests from the bed-and-breakfast. Walking toward them, I marvel again that Ninian's cross-lined cave should appeal to the wooly-haired sculptor. But he asks gruffly how I found the cave and tells of other times he has visited. The sculptor appears glad that I took his advice to come early; having seen me at the cave, the couple purposely delayed their approach in order to give me more time.

We say our farewells; then as I start to leave, he reaches up from his sitting position to offer me a thin, rectangular piece of slate on which he has been scratching away with a stone as we talked.

"This is a gift for you, David," he said, looking me in the eyes. I glance down and see that on the slate's smooth surface, the man whom I had pegged as a rough-hewn druid has etched with care a Celtic cross.

Stone Cross, Iona Abbey

Chapter 2

Iona and Saint Columba

"Stand fast"

If it is at all possible, stay at least one night on the island. Iona seems to hide her secrets from day-trippers, and can be wonderfully generous with those who stay awhile.

—DEBORAH

As I SCRAMBLE up the lee side of the hill through heather and grazing sheep, I am breathless and exhilarated, a little scared, and wet to the skin—although whether from rain or sea spray it is impossible to tell. I have never been out in a gale before, and a gale here on this tiny Hebridean island off the west coast of Scotland means more than a sixty-miles-per-hour wind—it blows right off the North Atlantic, elemental and wild, from just beyond the middle of nowhere.

This wind has already changed my life: I had planned to leave Iona this morning, but the storms have wrought havoc with the ferry schedules, and the locals only shrug when I ask when I will be able to return to the mainland. This is October; this is a remote and tiny island—I will leave when the weather permits and the Lord wills. I managed to telephone David and our daughters before the phone lines went out, so now I have nothing to do but play with the wind—or rather, let it play with me. For hours I have been swept before the wind, blown about like a leaf, from the abbey down to Columba's Bay and across the grassy, sandy reaches of the *machair* to the brow of this small hill.

The view from here is breathtaking in its timeless simplicity—rocks, heather, a wild chaos of surf at the far edge of the island, and then nothing but sea until it merges into sky.

I stand on Dun I (pronounced "Doon Ee"), the highest point on the island. When I reach the summit, the force of the wind, which the slope had tempered on my way up, actually knocks me down. When I regain my feet, I experiment with my balance and discover that I can literally lean on the wind, invisible but tangible as earth or stone. I rock forward on the balls of my feet and bank into the wind, arms out, head high, poised for a moment on the muscled air like a carved figurehead on a sailing ship, surrendered to the sky, plunging ahead into the storm.

I have a powerful sense of being where edges meet and disappear: horizon and shore are no tidy boundaries here but points of passionate encounter. The air is full of the salt and wet of the sea; the sea is whipped by the wild air; the earth is buffeted by sea and sky alike. The very sky seems lowering to touch the ground. Nothing is static; everything is in motion. I almost feel as though I am present at Creation before God separated the waters from the dry land. I definitely feel I am standing—precariously—on the very rim of the world.

I wonder if Saint Columba felt the same way. More than fourteen centuries have passed since that intrepid middle-aged Irish monk arrived on the island with his little band of followers—but he is the reason that I, like thousands of pilgrims before me, have come to Iona.

One of the great figures of the early history of Christianity in Britain and Ireland, Columba, of noble birth and monastic training, established a monastery on Iona about 563 C.E. (a century and a half after Saint Ninian at Whithorn) to bring the light of Christ to the Western Isles. From this minute rocky stronghold, that light would spread throughout modern Scotland and down into much of north and central England—years before Pope Gregory I sent Augustine, the archbishop of Canterbury, from Rome to convert the Anglo-Saxons in 597.

It is not clear why Columba left his beloved Ireland to start a new life in this wild place. Ancient records suggest political intrigue, possible exile. But whatever the particular reasons, such a journey would be consistent with the early Celtic tradition of setting out as wandering pilgrims to find the place of one's own resurrection. Like the desert fathers and mothers of Egypt, who strongly influenced early Irish monasticism, Celtic Christians often sought out isolated, barren places on the edge of the world to offer themselves to God so deeply as to receive as gift from the risen Christ their own spiritual death and rebirth.

Legend has it that Columba and his followers left Ireland in a small fleet of *curraghs* or coracles—small, round boats made of willow and animal hide, with neither rudder nor sail, totally surrendered to the current and wind for direction. Thus "abandoned to divine Providence" they eventually landed on Iona and—after climbing a hill to be sure they were out of sight of the beloved Ireland they had left behind—decided that this was where they would stay. As I lean into the wild wind at the top of Dun I, I can imagine their sense of having found, as Mendelssohn described it in 1829 when he visited Iona, "the loneliest loneliness" in the world.

However, it is important not to oversimplify or romanticize those distant days. *Peregrinatio,* or pilgrimage, certainly had connotations of exile, renunciation, searching for God in the wilderness—but Columba and his monks neither sought nor found an escape from the world. In the first place, "monasteries were almost certainly the busiest institutions in Celtic society, constantly teeming with people and fulfilling the roles of school, library, hospital, guest house, arts centre and mission station."[1] More importantly, the ancient notion of pilgrimage was not one primarily of flight to the edge but of return to the center: the earliest Christian pilgrimages were transforming journeys to Jerusalem, the *axis mundi,* the very center of the world. One left stability behind and headed for the place where edges meet, in order to find the heart of things.[2]

Columba, revered as a saint for both active and contemplative values, seems to have combined a passionate mystical solitude with phenomenal missionary zeal: after his death he was honored as *cet cell custoit—* guardian of a hundred churches.

Scholarly opinion divides on whether Columba and those early monks saw themselves as hermits or as missionaries—perhaps they lived as both. What can seem from the outside to be paradox is often experienced as balance, and the mystics report that the stillness at the heart of God is both our destination and the grace by which we seek it. Living at the edge may also be all about living from the center. As T. S. Eliot reminds us, "At the still point of the turning world" there is "neither from nor towards . . . neither arrest nor movement"—only the light, "a white light still and moving."[3]

It is that radiant, dynamic stillness that we seek whenever we step away from where we are—it may look like the very edge of the world, but it is also home. Perhaps Columba knew himself to be truly standing at the brink of everything and—simultaneously—rooted at the heart of it.

Almost as abandoned to the whim of the wind as if I were attempting to navigate a coracle through the sea, I allow myself to be blown back down the lee side of Dun I and across the island again, south to Columba's Bay. One of the remarkable things about Iona is apparent here: a geologic footnote that adds to the aura of the island's ancient mystery—the age of the rock from which it is made. Apparently the stone of Iona is among the oldest on the surface of the planet—thrust up eons ago from the very depths of the primordial sea. No fossil record exists here—this rock predates all life. Once there was a small marble quarry here, long since abandoned. The pebbled beach is strewn with fragments of white marble, polished into roundness by centuries of wind and sea. These mingle with tumbled bits of quartz, feldspar, hornblende, slate, and epidote. The ones I like best are silvery green streaked with white, locally known as "Columba's tears." But the sea today is an awesome thing—the spray hurls itself a hundred feet in the air and stings like a whip. This is no day to linger by the shore. Quickly I choose a pebble from the beach and thrust it into my pocket.

It will, however, take more than stones in my pockets to hinder the wind's having its way with me. Turning north from the bay means turning back to face the wind, and I fight for every step of the two miles back across the island to the grounds of the restored medieval abbey. To walk this way is, for a while, to be completely out of sight of the abbey and the tiny village on the eastern shore—to lose, as John L. Paterson has pointed out,

> all sight of human occupation and to be aware of the three elements—earth, sky and sea—which not only provide a constant reflection on the temporal nature of man, but also an awareness of infinity. There are other parts of the island which are possibly more beautiful but none that suggests with such directness the inconsequence of time as a measure of existence.[4]

I battle my way, yard by stormy yard, past the grazing pasture called Eithne's Fold, where the monks kept their sheep. I press on past the remains of the ancient Augustinian nunnery, built in the early thirteenth century by Reginald, son of Somerled, Lord of the Isles. Nearly tempted to drop to the ground and crawl by now, I stagger past Oran's Chapel and across the *Reilig Oran,* ancient burial ground of sixty kings—Scottish, Irish, and Norwegian—including, it is said, Duncan and his murderer, Macbeth. These are some of the most famous, most atmospheric places on Iona. But I am seeking refuge from atmosphere at the moment, and I struggle with the church's heavy doors until at last I stand in the comparative quiet of the nave.

Inside the abbey, a group of tourists moves toward the altar at the east end of the church, so I—seeking shelter but not company—duck into a low doorway and up a dark and winding stone staircase to the tower. The narrow lancet windows are unglazed, and the ubiquitous wind roars into the space and whirls downward in a mighty draft. As I grasp at a stone window ledge for balance, I wonder what recklessness or sheer contrariness keeps me, in a gale on a flat island, obstinately seeking the highest points around rather than prudently lying low until the storm is over. Once again I wonder if this isn't part of the spell of Iona, this longing for higher ground something Columba himself might have felt. I remember a verse of a psalm: "Lead me to the rock that is higher than I; For thou hast been a shelter for me, and a strong tower from the enemy" (Ps. 61:2-3, KJV).

Even in the relative shelter of the tower, the wind whips my hair about my face and flaps the sleeves of my nylon rain jacket as though they were sails. As I stand braced against the sill of the narrow window, I notice what is carved into the stone lintel above it: "Stand fast."

As I make my way back down the corkscrew stairs, riding the current of captured wind like a cork in a whirlpool, I salute the memory of all the monks across the windswept centuries who have, in this remote and barren place of austere blessing, indeed stood fast—lived hidden lives of faith, rooted in God and abandoned to the wind of the Spirit.

Long intrigued by the flowing lines and mysterious symbols of Celtic design, I have pored over ancient illuminated manuscripts and fragments of carved stone in museums in Ireland and Scotland. But those glimpses had not prepared me for the experience of actually standing in front of one of the huge carved freestanding crosses on the grounds of the abbey. One of these, Saint Martin's Cross, dates from the early eighth century and offers a marvelous example of its kind: massive Irish granite, twelve to fourteen feet tall, beautifully carved with intricate designs, a circle joining the intersecting arms of the cross. It stands where it has stood for a thousand years, resolute against gales, Vikings, and Victorian vandals. In the brutal winds of this October storm, I am tempted literally to cling to the cross—and in that longing I receive, for a moment, another insight into the paradox of living on the edge and moving from the center—a glimpse into what it might mean to "stand fast."

A radiant conviction of the "real presence" of Christ and all the angels and saints is one of the most striking aspects of Celtic Christian spirituality: the Cross stands firmly at the heart of that tradition, as deeply rooted and as steadfast in endurance as the stone cross standing before me. The Christian Celtic tradition is also characterized by the paradox I have felt so keenly on Iona: the stillness at the heart of the journey into God, the trust and peacefulness in the midst of the tumult. A line of an ancient prayer occurs to me now:

May the shelter I seek
be the shadow of your cross.[5]

Perhaps the key to the riddle lies, more than I had supposed, in the great stone crosses that stand like sentinels in the wind-scoured land. Perhaps it is only in clinging to the cross of Christ, in finding our only true shelter standing fast beneath its arms, that we can hope to live either on the edge or from the center.

〜

It is night, but still the gale roars. The restored medieval abbey, where a handful of pilgrims has gathered for evening prayer, is lit only by candles inside wrought iron sconces. Even within their glass chimneys, the flames tremble in the wind that cannot be kept out. In this flickering darkness, in the penetrating, drafty cold of an autumn night, it is only too easy to imagine life here in the fifteenth century, when the medieval abbey church was rebuilt under the auspices of Abbot Dominic.

Only traces remain in the north transept of the earlier church built by Reginald on this site in 1203—there are no traces at all of the church Queen Margaret is thought to have built here in 1072, restoring the earlier monastic foundation after the savage destruction caused by repeated Viking attacks from 794 to 986. Of the daub-and-wattle buildings erected by Columba, not a straw remains.

Columba's legacy was a tenacious one, however; for centuries the monastic community he founded maintained its spiritual leadership in the Western Isles. It was not until 1638 that the last bishop of Iona was deposed, ending 1075 years of a continuing line of Columba's successors. After that, the abbey gradually fell into decay. By the middle of the nineteenth century, sentimental Victorian sightseers, chipping off bits of the high altar as souvenirs, had completed the ruin of the great church, among whose broken walls the islanders' cattle grazed. It seemed that the first part of Columba's own prophecy had been fulfilled:

Iona of my heart,
Iona of my love,

Instead of monks' voices
Shall be the lowing of cattle.[6]

However, in 1938 the Iona Community, under the formidable leadership of George MacLeod, a visionary minister of the Church of Scotland, undertook the daunting project of restoring the abbey.[7]

The intention of the Community was not only to repair the fabric of the ancient buildings as a symbol of the conjunction of the spiritual and the material in modern life but also to create on Iona a center from which to take those principles into the world. Presently, the Iona Community has an interdenominational, international membership of thousands. Their goal is not to recreate monastic life but to commit themselves to one another in the context of their ordinary lives, bound by a common discipline of prayer and work. The Community supports the abbey not as a museum but as a living house of prayer.

Participating in worship on that dark and stormy night, I could believe the final part of Columba's prophecy to be fulfilled at last:

But ere the world comes to an end,
Iona shall be as it was.[8]

Tonight the ancient and enduring faith of those sixth-century monks burns in this place like a flame, more steadfast than the quaking candles in the choir, more robust in its silent witness than our thin voices raised above the wind.

I kneel in the choir and pray, "May the shelter I seek be the shadow of your cross."

Upon waking the next morning, the first thing I notice is the silence. The wind still breathes (I wonder if it ever stops here) but in the merest sighing whisper compared to the groaning, screaming clamor of the past two days. The storm is over.

My farewell walk across the island this morning is the most sedate and uneventful of strolls compared to the elemental tug-of-war it was yesterday. The sky is a rinsed and milky blue in which, high above the earth again, dove-grey wisps of cloud are moving. The sea no longer fills the air but stretches out where it belongs, iron grey ruffled with white. Earth, sky, and sea are separate again; once more the elements keep their appointed places. As I walk through the village, I see the jetty stirring with life again, preparing for the resumed ferry service across the mile of sea between Iona and Mull.

I climb to the top of Dun I and find (almost to my disappointment) that I can stand upright on the summit, this time neither bowled over nor held aloft by the powerful air. I find in my jacket pocket the small, smooth stone I picked up on the beach the day before, and I finger it idly, thinking about Columba and his monks who lived here in the sixth century, about the Augustinian nuns who lived here in the Middle Ages, about George MacLeod and his stubborn dreams of restoration, about all the faithful who have ever sought the edge of the world in order to find the center. I remember my earlier visit to this small hill, exhilarating and a bit alarming in the sheer force of the elements, the sense of being where edges meet and disappear.

I am beginning to realize that living on the edge involves us in constantly moving on: the horizon disappears as we approach it, is revealed in fact to be an illusion. There is no edge. There is no end. The sphere is unbounded. There is only the still point of the turning world. Our only hope of wholeness lies in the dynamic integration offered us by the Cross—there can be no stasis, no escape, no fixity. Only a joyful ever-moving-on where the winds of the Spirit take us, secure only in the knowledge that wherever we are, God is with us.

As Thomas Merton said,

> We cannot arrive at the perfect possession of God in this life, and that is why we are travelling. . . . But we already possess [God] by grace, and therefore in that sense we have arrived.
>
> . . . But oh! How far have I to go to find You in Whom I have already arrived![9]

Near the summit of Dun I, not a yard from where I stand, a heap of stones rises taller than I am—a cairn, or memorial marker, spontaneously created at sacred places by those who make pilgrimage to them. I gaze at the cairn for a long time, wondering how many thousands of stones compose it, holding in prayer all the people who have traveled to this place and marked their presence in such a small, concrete, and anonymous way. I realize this cairn represents a whole communion of saints, a community of people to which I belong, although I will never meet them or even know who they are.

Carefully I add my stone to the pile and head on down the slope again—strengthened by my time in this place, light of heart and hopeful of the grace to stand fast and move on, ever deeper into the God in whom we have already arrived.

Lindisfarne from St. Cuthbert's Island

Chapter 3

The Holy Island of Lindisfarne and Saints Aidan & Cuthbert

"A place more venerable than all in Britain"

To trace the origins of Christianity in northern England is to return to Lindisfarne. Even if the priory's ruins were ground to dust, visitors would still cross to Holy Island at low tide to feel the wind, heed the eternal, and hear of lives singularly attentive to God.

—David

*I*TRAVELED TO LINDISFARNE, drawn by the promise of priory ruins and an island linked at odd hours to England. Often veiled in ocean haze, it rises out of the North Sea three miles off the Northumberland coast. Here on the ragged edge of the world, Lindisfarne became a beacon for Christianity in northern England. The eighth-century scholar Alcuin called it "a place more venerable than all in Britain."[1] Through a windy mix of landscape and biography, Lindisfarne has oriented visitors toward God for more than thirteen hundred years.

"As the tide ebbs and flows," explained Saint Bede, "this place is surrounded by sea twice a day like an island, and twice a day the sand dries and joins it to the mainland."[2] The approach to Lindisfarne, as with Cornwall's Saint Michael's Mount or Normandy's Mont-Saint-Michel, can be narrow and fleeting; fast-rising tides have at times trapped incautious travelers. Visitors can cross the glistening mud flats only from three hours after high tide until two hours before it. Ancient pilgrims did so by foot, following stone cairns (now replaced by fourteen-foot-high wooden guideposts). Most contemporary visitors glance at their watches, however, and choose instead to reach Lindisfarne by car, negotiating a slender, paved causeway lined with drying kelp.

Though posted tide tables now advise safe crossing times, a passage nevertheless demands attention. For those heedless of tides, emergency "refuge boxes"—three wooden huts accessible by ladders—perch on pillars like tree houses above the seafloor.

Known also as Holy Island since the eleventh century, Lindisfarne remains the more ancient, unique, and telling name. *Lindis* stems from the title of a nearby stream, while *farne*—possibly meaning "a place of retreat" in Celtic tradition—suggests what the island has provided visitors through the centuries.

Leaving the mainland, I cross the ribbon of causeway in minutes, then reach the island's outlying salt marshes and sand dunes. Driving past a handful of cottages and a gentle rise of fertile fields, I arrive in the snug village of Lindisfarne, its population of 150 now dependent as much on tourism as fishing and farming. Tucked in the small island's southwest corner, the hamlet seems to encroach on its ancient Benedictine priory as though seeking heat from the hearth that once warmed Northumbrians.

I leave my overnight bag at a bed-and-breakfast, then stop quickly for tea and scones at a cafe, bolting them so rapidly the proprietor looks at me with astonishment. "Why, you couldn't have tasted them," she says. "You're on the island now. You can slow down." Barely mindful of her advice, I walk quickly past the village's cluster of sea-bitten houses and craft shops. As I approach the medieval priory, its broken profile of red sandstone emerges at last through the late morning haze.

Little remains of the twelfth-century Benedictine priory: a quarter of its nave, roofless transepts and towers, remnants of walls sanded by sea wind, the stone softened, worn, frayed, and fluted. The rose-red sandstone, reminiscent of canyon rock in the American Southwest, here has been carved into arches and crosses for the glory of God. A spectacular transverse arch with dog-tooth ornament soars between grey sky and green turf. "Durham Cathedral in miniature," earlier visitors have exclaimed, instinctively recognizing the priory's link to artisans and Benedictines from Durham who crafted these stones.

Though less exquisite a ruin than the soaring Rievaulx Abbey or Fountains Abbey, there is a sense of a far older sanctuary here, more ancient than the visible Norman stone. The windburned walls evoke memories of even earlier missionaries and lives of austerity, risk, and proclamation. Of that first Celtic church nothing remains. No walls of timber or roofs of thatch. Nothing except the story.

Invited by the mainland king to introduce Christianity to his raw Northumbrian realm, Aidan arrived in 635 from Iona, bringing the torch of Saint Columba's monastic settlement to another holy island. Aidan "cultivated peace and love, purity and humility," noted Bede in his *Ecclesiastical History of the English People.* He "used his priestly authority to check the proud and powerful; he tenderly comforted the sick; he relieved and protected the poor."[3] Journeying out often from this island monastery to baptize and teach, Aidan helped tame barbarism, persuading warring tribes to lay down their weapons.

A twentieth-century statue of Aidan, backed by a Celtic cross, stands near a grove of wind-bent sycamores and whitebeam trees. Gaunt, visionary, and fearless, his sculpted countenance alone can cause visitors to muse, *So this is how Christianity spread.* As tenacious as Ninian at Whithorn and Columba at Iona, Aidan was "a man of outstanding gentleness, holiness, and moderation."[4]

Bede may have overstated; the temptation to view saints through lenses as rose-colored as Lindisfarne's arches can be matched by a tendency to disparage the faith of contemporaries. What would be an unremarkable lament from a twenty-first-century observer—"His life is in marked contrast to the apathy of our own times"—originates from the eighth-century Bede himself.[5] The way out, of course, is to put full confidence neither in Bede nor Aidan but in the One to whom they both gave witness.

Both Aidan and a later bishop of Lindisfarne, Cuthbert (c. 634–87), left an unblemished legacy. Ex-shepherd, former mainland missionary, and guardian of seabirds, Cuthbert bracketed his Lindisfarne tenure with even deeper solitude on the neighboring Farne Islands. "Above all else," wrote Bede, "he was afire with heavenly love, unassumingly patient, devoted to unceasing prayer, and kindly to all who came to him for comfort."[6] Miracles associated with Cuthbert's life and his incorruptible remains helped usher in the long centuries of pilgrimage to Lindisfarne.

Bede also confirmed that Cuthbert evinced "a love for proclaiming his message."[7] The story of Jesus often hinges on proclamation. "So faith comes from what is heard," wrote Paul, "and what is heard comes by the preaching of Christ" (Rom. 10:17, RSV).

Except in the wake of someone's words, the priory would be mute, its cross incomprehensible.

The monks of Lindisfarne often ventured forth to preach and baptize throughout northern England. Returning here, they would be nourished again with prayer, liturgy, and spiritual discipline. After a time, in a rhythm reminiscent of the tides themselves, they would gather their bearings and cross the sands again, their voices emboldened.

Across the cloister, a band of schoolchildren, sketchpads in hand, surveys the remains of a stone bench used in the monastic kitchen. As wind roils through the priory, several boys climb low walls enclosing the ancient warming room. Their teacher checks his watch; the tide leaves them little time to linger. Finishing their drawings, the children leave as silence reclaims the ruins.

Divine grace tends to be caught in broken cisterns, and by the late Middle Ages the monastery had succumbed to lax ways, far from Aidan and Cuthbert's beginnings. The priory's clouded history checks us from confusing holy islands with holiness itself, as though one could trap God in sacred space. As author Belden Lane reminds visitors to sacred places: "God is *here*—in this place at Bethlehem, Lourdes, Iona, etc. But, at the same time, God is *not* here—not limited exclusively to this place, not *only* here."[8]

Wind snatches at the last two tourists to enter before a staff member of English Heritage closes the priory for the day. We are part of the early lapping wave of travelers, not yet summer's high tide that will bring thousands a day to Holy Island, once northern England's prime pilgrimage destination. Now visitors with pilgrim hearts often hide behind tourist masks of curiosity, as the wind brings to mind a story of faith partly forgotten or never learned.

———

To the east, half a mile away across the flat island, Lindisfarne Castle spirals into the sky from a spur of basalt. Irresistible to photographers because of its soaring eminence, the castle ironically has begun to supplant the Benedictine monastery on the cover of contemporary publications about Holy Island.

In a secular eclipse of the spiritual, the sixteenth-century garrison—built with stones cannibalized from the priory—tends to overshadow the monastic ruins on many visitors' itineraries as well. Snug against the wind, cozy as castles go, the citadel was built to defend the harbor, then restored by Sir Edwin Lutyens into a private residence now owned by the National Trust.

Yet after a brief tour of the stronghold's low-ceilinged, compact quarters, I encounter a familiar paradox: A tour of a fortress tires me, while a visit to a roofless priory somehow fortifies. Over the centuries, paths of pilgrims have tended to lead away from castles, not toward them.

It is possible to walk around the island (roughly 1½ miles from north to south and a mile from east to west) in a few hours, but its wilder north coast of crescent bays and grey seal colonies remains largely unvisited. ("You'll feel like you're on the edge of the world, it's so windy," a young woman, island native, promises me.)

Naturalist Richard Perry claimed that Holy Island offered "undreamt of" opportunities for bird-watching.[9] Even more abundant birdlife thrives on the neighboring Farne Islands, an archipelago of dolerite rocks seven miles southeast of Lindisfarne. Few places in the world harbor more seabirds in such a small setting, the breeding ground for more than twenty species—including cormorant, kittiwake, tern, sea duck, and puffin—now protected by the National Trust.

Lifeboats once set sail from the Farne Islands to pluck the shipwrecked to safety. Indeed, one of the nation's most dramatic rescues occurred when the lighthouse keeper's twenty-two-year-old daughter (the aptly named Grace Darling) rowed through a storm to save survivors from the wrecked *Forfarshire,* her courage electrifying nineteenth-century England.

Cuthbert's thirst for solitude eventually led him to a hermitage on one of the Farne Islands, where he built a circular cell of stones and turf, roofed by timbers. In a typically Celtic manner, he cast his protective mantle around more than humans: credited as the first person in Britain to protect birds, he laid down rules for the safety of eider ducks nesting on the Farne Islands, initiating a sanctuary for seabirds that continues to this day.

Cuthbert spent a lifetime telling others of God's grace. It is perhaps not surprising that the Farne Islands themselves, bane of ships and shelter for seabirds, retain a legacy of rescue and redemption as well.

In honor "of God and Cuthbert," a successor bishop at Lindisfarne in 700 crafted the Lindisfarne Gospels. Akin to Ireland's Book of Kells, the 259 folio pages of vellum offer a masterpiece of manuscript illumination, brilliantly ornamented with forty-five different colors mixed with egg yolk to keep the text from flaking. Written in Latin, with interlinear notation in Northumbrian dialect added about 250 years later, the Lindisfarne Gospels represent the earliest surviving translation of all four Gospels into a form of English.

Having survived harrowing travel and a sea drenching, the illuminated manuscript now rests securely under glass in London's British Library, not far from the Codex Sinaiticus and the original score to the Beatles' "A Hard Day's Night." On Holy Island, Lindisfarne's parish church displays a twentieth-century facsimile edition, while the Lindisfarne

Heritage Centre offers an electronic, interactive version of the Gospels, which allows visitors to turn pages by touching a computer screen.

Superlatives adorn the manuscript, and the book itself has become more widely known than its original island home. Though no more effective than a Gideon's Bible in conveying the story of Christ, the Lindisfarne Gospels remain one of the world's most beautiful works of art, and testimony to a man's response to the words within.

As a bell sounds for evensong in the parish church, I take a seat in the twilit chapel with four other parishioners. The vicar of Holy Island, David Adam, well-known for his books on Celtic spirituality, leads us in antiphonal readings as the wind outside submerges our voices. Few places in Britain have held services more continuously. Except for the years when bloody Viking raids depopulated Lindisfarne (and bequeathed the title Holy Island in honor of slain monks), prayers like tonight's final prayer have been uttered here on evenings since 635:

> Lighten our darkness, we beseech thee, O Lord;
> and by thy great mercy defend us
> from all perils and dangers of this night;
> for the love of thy only Son,
> our Saviour, Jesus Christ. Amen.[10]

By chance we sit together by gender, three men on one side, three women on the other, our eyes unmeeting. The sparse attendance does not surprise me, given Holy Island's few homes and guest bedrooms, but for a moment we seem only a distant echo of robust Celtic vesper services. Then I catch myself: I am not immune from the infection that enfeebles worship services everywhere—regret over the absent rather than gratitude for those present.

After evensong, with wind gusts snapping at my jacket and seagulls whirling overhead, I climb a path behind the church to the Heugh, a grass-covered dolerite ridge some two hundred yards long. Though only fifty feet high, it offers a spectacular vista over most of the island and a gull's-eye view down into the priory itself.

In the empty, gated quarters, shadows stretch across the cloister, draining the stones of color. Beside the priory in a dark green field, grazing sheep cast long shadows in the low sun. I sit on a bench along the ridge, sheltered from the wind by a rock wall.

I put away the guidebooks, pamphlets, and Bede's chronicles: no more dates, narratives, or diagrams of ecclesial architecture. With an intake of breath, I remind myself why I have come: to step across the threshold of retreat.

For a few moments my mind continues to dart with ideas, frenetic as the swallows above the cloister. Slowly I become quiet, the stillness primed in part by three questions once posed by Saint Ignatius: "What have I done for Christ? What am I doing for Christ? What ought I to do for Christ?"[11] Beyond that I at last reach silence and prayer.

To the west now, tidal sands no longer glint in twilight. The rising sea has begun to cast off Holy Island from England. Tomorrow morning when the ocean recedes, new visitors will arrive, attentive and expectant in the wind-honed silence. Others like myself will leave Lindisfarne, paralleling the route taken by Aidan and Cuthbert. The cairns guiding the Celtic saints, like today's guideposts and causeway, lead away from the island no less than toward it. Midway across the tidal sands, we will glance back for a final view. As the name itself suggests, Lindisfarne remains a place of retreat, apart yet linked, as we return to the mainland of our lives.

Memorial Window, St. Margaret's Chapel, Edinburgh Castle

Chapter 4

St. Margaret's Chapel and Saint Margaret

"Faith built upon the rock"

If you can find a moment between waves of castle tourists to slip into the chapel when it is quiet and empty, you may sense the ancient peace still breathing from the stones.

—DEBORAH

*I*T IS RAINING, inevitably, on the wintry morning I have chosen to explore Edinburgh Castle. I don't mind, though; the weather has discouraged other visitors, and it suits the place—there would be something incongruous, almost frivolous, about this grim and brooding fortress, stone built on solid stone, on a merely sunny day.

So I have the place to myself as I wander in the rain through the gatehouse, up the great curving cobbled roads past batteries and barracks. At the very heart of the castle precincts, at the highest pinnacle of Castle Rock, is the small building I have come to see: St. Margaret's Chapel, freestanding, plain, and unpretentious as it has stood for nearly nine centuries, the oldest surviving part of the castle, the oldest building in all this venerable city, and the oldest Norman church in Scotland.

It is tiny—twenty people would be a snug fit—and as resonant and empty as a seashell. The graceful lines of vaulted roof and rounded door and windows relieve the rectangular austerity. A marvelous Norman archway divides the small nave from the even smaller semicircular vaulted apse on the east side. A bouquet of fresh flowers adorns the altar.

It is very lovely. I am, in fact, taken aback by the palpable peace and beauty of the space. Rain hisses against the narrow windows, but otherwise the silence is unbroken, and profound. I can easily imagine the young queen (1047–93) here in this place she loved, a tiny island of prayer in the tumultuous sea of castle life.

It has not always been so peaceful here. Edinburgh Castle was the focal point for political and military turmoil in Scotland for nearly a thousand years; many times throughout the centuries these walls have rung with the noise of battle. In 1314 they also rang to the sounds of demolition: Thomas Randolph, Scottish Earl of Moray, having brilliantly recaptured the castle from under the noses of the sleeping English garrison, and unwilling to let the prize of the castle fall again into enemy hands, ordered every building in the castle razed—except St. Margaret's Chapel. On his deathbed in 1329, another Scottish hero, King Robert I the Bruce, spoke of the lonely chapel on the desolate rock and set aside money for the repair of its broken windows.

These round-headed windows, set in stone walls two feet thick, echo the shape of the wooden entrance door as well as the magnificent Norman arch that separates the minute chancel from the nave. Some say David I, Margaret's son, may have built the chapel as a memorial to his mother, as he founded the Abbey of the Holy Rood in her memory. Others think that the chapel itself is older—old enough to be the very oratory that her biographer mentions as Margaret's constant refuge, which she sought night and day for prayer, where she attended Mass and received Communion on the day she died.

Standing here, I can hardly believe it was not her own. The small enclosed space within these walls feels as surely shaped by prayer as the Norman arch was carved in stone.

It is remarkable that the prayerful atmosphere should linger still, since—although records of use of the "Chapel Royal" occur through-out the Middle Ages—from the sixteenth century it seems the build-ing was used for anything but prayer. It was only rediscovered in 1845, at which time it was being used as the powder magazine of the Argyle Battery. Sir Daniel Wilson, who conducted his renovations at the request of Queen Victoria, reported that "the gunpowder was stored in the apse; the little round-headed window on its south side was built up; and the garrison chapel, a plain unsightly modern build-ing, which then stood immediately to the east, effectively blocked up the central window."[1]

These narrow windows—so carefully restored in the fourteenth cen-tury at the order of a dying king, and so carelessly obscured by mili-tary pragmatism in the eighteenth and nineteenth centuries—are once again both glazed and whole. Douglas Strachan designed the lovely stained-glass windows that were installed in the 1920s—the one be-hind the altar in the east wall shows Saint Andrew, patron saint of Scotland; the one in the western wall a bit incongruously depicts Sir William Wallace, a favorite Scottish hero of the thirteenth century (but not one usually remembered for his holiness). To the delight of my Celtic heart, the three windows in the south wall commemorate respectively Saint Ninian, Saint Columba, and—of course—Saint Margaret her-self, depicted as a calm and handsome woman with a golden crown atop thick flaxen plaits, seated, with a book in her hands.

―――

Margaret's guide and confessor was a priest named Turgot (later prior of Durham, finally bishop of St. Andrews). At the request of Margaret's daughter Matilda (then queen of England, having married Henry I in 1100), Turgot wrote *The Life of Saint Margaret* just over a decade after Margaret's death. This remarkable document—strong and resolute hagiography—omits much that we would like to know, but it re-mains the primary source for our knowledge of Margaret's life and death.

Turgot, no doubt mindful of his audience but clearly persuaded of Margaret's holiness, assures Matilda that "nothing was firmer than [her mother's] fidelity, steadier than her favour, or juster than her decisions, nothing more enduring than her patience, graver than her advice or more pleasant than her conversation."[2]

A summary of *The Life* sounds much like a fairy tale: Once upon a time, a beautiful and devout Saxon princess, a *de facto* exile from England after the Norman Conquest in 1066, was shipwrecked off the coast of Scotland—possibly fleeing north toward Norway. She was rescued by the barbarian King Malcolm, who fell in love with the homeless princess; they were married within the year. She—like a proper fairy-tale princess—was as good as she was beautiful. She won the wild hearts of Scottish nobility and peasantry alike by her passion for justice and mercy, and her love of the church. She brought the order and discipline of Roman liturgy to the haphazard local practice, and inspired court and clergy by her care of the poor. Her practical charity was outmatched only by her personal devotion: she attended every hour of worship, observed all fast days, and devoted herself to hours of private prayer. She bore eight children and raised them to be themselves good kings and queens. She died at the age of forty-six, holding a cross, a prayer on her lips.

Beyond the fairy tale—which is actually grounded in historical fact—lie the criticism and the controversy. Some assessments of Saint Margaret (who was canonized in 1250 C.E., incidentally one of the rare female saints who was neither virgin nor widow but the happy mother of a large family) disparage her as a "severe lady, who checked mirth at court and dominated her husband."[3] One eminent Scottish historian has rather snidely suggested that Malcolm "offset the oppressive piety of his household by four times invading the north of England."[4] Another has pointed out that "the young queen had no very high standards to live up to, her predecessor being Lady Macbeth."[5]

More seriously, views differ on the value of Margaret's contribution to church history. On the one hand, she is lauded for introducing far-reaching changes into worship and practice, bringing the "barbarian North" into the Roman fold; on the other hand, she has been harshly criticized for initiating the destruction of indigenous Celtic

Christianity. It would appear that in fact the truth lies, as it so often does, somewhere in between.

—

It seems fitting that here in St. Margaret's Chapel at the heart of Edinburgh Castle, the stained-glass window depicting Saint Margaret should be right next to the one honoring Saint Columba. A strong tradition links Saint Margaret with Iona: when the Western Isles, for many years in the hands of Norway, came under Malcolm's protection in 1072, Queen Margaret sent money to restore the monastery there from Viking depredations. I feel sure that Columba and Margaret, although separated by several turbulent centuries and hailing from two different cultures, would have recognized instantly in each other a kindred love of God and the church. In both of them, great personal sanctity was allied with persuasive charm and formidable organizational ability; both are rightly revered as jewels in Scotland's Christian crown.

Nevertheless, by Margaret's day, Columba had been dead for centuries, and his legacy was growing dim: the church he and the great Celtic pioneers left behind had grown stagnant, isolated, and weak. The religious heirs of Columba (known as "Culdees" from the Gaelic *Céli Dé,* "companions of God") still lived in the traditional small communities of twelve or less, under an abbot or prior as superior. But by Margaret's time, these monastic clergy were still the only clergy in the land, and they lived isolated lives of prayer with little regard for the pastoral needs of the people, and no sense of connection with the life of the church elsewhere.

Margaret was a nobly born, gently bred, highly educated, religiously observant young woman; she had been born into a highly cultured Christian court in Hungary and raised in another in England. So when forced to flee the English court after the advent of William the Conqueror, she must have been dismayed to find herself in the wilds of Scotland, and disturbed by the state of church and court. As queen she would naturally have felt some obligation to do what she could to improve both religious observance and pastoral care for the poor.

At any rate, sometime after 1070—soon after her marriage to Malcolm—Margaret approached Lanfranc, then archbishop of Canterbury, for help in reforming the church in Scotland. She also seems to have been instrumental in organizing and even moderating the famous three-day council, probably held in St. Andrews[6] about 1074, that attempted to reconcile the differences between the Culdees and the Roman church.[7]

It is interesting to note, in the context of accusations sometimes brought against Margaret for destroying the distinctive character of "Celtic Christianity," just how small the agenda for this council really was. There seem to have been only a small handful of issues at stake, and none of them strike modern ears as theologically or politically explosive. Like the questions that had earlier concerned the Synod of Whitby in 664 C.E., the debate was not over doctrine but discipline.[8]

The most apparently substantive point of the council involved the liturgy of the Mass: Margaret and the delegation from Canterbury wanted conformity here with the Latin liturgy rather than "after a barbarous ritual." Tantalizingly, there is no way to know what this phrase means—had the Culdees been saying Mass in Gaelic rather than Latin? We may never know. At any rate, Turgot's record of the council does not reflect cultural imperialism so much as a modest desire to bring the isolated Culdee practice more explicitly in line with what the rest of the Christian world was doing. Again, as at Whitby four hundred years earlier, the goal was merely to establish a universal rather than a local practice for Christian life and worship.

In any event, it does not seem that there was much opposition: Turgot reports that "no one on the opposite side could say one word against them [Margaret's proposals]; nay, rather, giving up their obstinacy and yielding to reason, they willingly consented to adopt all she recommended."[9]

Far from being at inquisitional pains to correct the errors of the Culdees, Margaret clearly admired them; she not only sent funds for the restoration of Iona but also maintained close friendships with many of the *Céli Dé*, visiting them in their monasteries and discussing religious matters with them, seeking their counsel, giving them generous grants of land and money, and encouraging them in their transcribing of sacred books.[10] Margaret did, soon after her marriage in the little Culdee church in Dunfermline, replace the small existing building with the large, fine Holy Trinity Abbey, built in the Norman manner, more in keeping with the Roman usage she sought to introduce. However, she did not displace the Culdee clergy, and built the new church over the old one, so the ancient site was both honored and preserved as a place of worship. Through a grille over a hole cut in the stone floor, one can still see a bit of the floor of the eleventh-century church built on Margaret's orders, testimony to both change and continuity across the ages.

The record is undisputed that whatever her role as a reformer, Margaret was a great lover of God and extravagant in her love, for Christ's sake, of the poor. She seems to have longed, within the context of life with her family and at court, with all her activity in affairs of both church and state, to live the life of a Benedictine nun. According to Turgot, she prayed the divine office every day and was passionate in the practices of hospitality and almsgiving. Turgot tells us that during the liturgical seasons of Advent and Lent, she not only fed nine orphan children every morning, taking them on her knee and feeding them tenderly with her own spoon, but that afterward, she and Malcolm would personally feed three hundred poor people, "waiting upon Christ in the person of His poor." Even if, as may well be, this number is exaggerated, there is no reason to doubt that the royal household did indeed provide food and drink to many—and as Margaret's biographer Lucy Menzies says, "The description of the warlike Malcolm, the proud King of Scots, waiting on the poor down one side of the hall while the queen waited on the other, shows us the extent of her conquest."[11]

Margaret's historical and ecclesial significance aside, I have always been intrigued and amused by her legendary conquest of Malcolm. A portrait of Queen Margaret and King Malcolm, which now hangs in

Dunfermline, has become one of my favorite images of Margaret.[12] It nicely portrays Victorian piety and values: The young and lovely queen, gracefully draped in embroidered silk with a jeweled circlet on her flowing red-gold hair, sits on a stone by a wooded stream beside her husband. A book lies on her knee, and she is obviously telling him the story of the gospel. Her face is rapt, her eyes fixed on an unseen point in the distance. Her slender white hand lies affectionately on his big brown fist. Malcolm sits beside her, clothed in the chain mail and leather, crown and sword of his warrior-kingly calling, leaning his rough head in his hand and gazing respectfully down at the book, every line of his figure indicating his rude strength, his touching devotion to his bride, and his bewildered, illiterate attempt to understand what she is saying.

The book in the painting is Margaret's famous Gospel book—also pictured in the stained-glass window in the chapel in Edinburgh Castle—around which some of the most charming legends about Margaret have grown. One tale recounts, for instance, how the book once fell into a stream and was rescued from the water undamaged and quite dry. Turgot also tells us, in a sweet vignette that offers another unusual glimpse of Malcolm, the erstwhile "scourge of the North," that the king was so in love with his young queen and so in awe of her learning and her piety that he had her book beautifully bound and jeweled, and although he himself could neither read nor write, he used to pick it up and reverently kiss it for her sake.[13]

From the cobbled space now immediately in front of Margaret's Chapel—where the royal residence probably stood in the eleventh century—the steep northern face of Castle Mound drops dramatically away into what was once the Nor' Loch, a lake built, like a moat, between the castle and the sea to protect the castle from invasions. Now, hundreds of feet below, the velvety green of Edinburgh's Princes Street Gardens unfurls between the castle and the New Town, the railroad tracks running through it like a river. Princes Street is alive with bobbing black umbrellas; double-decker buses streak their red against the grey.

This spot commands a marvelous view of the largely eighteenth-century "New Town" below, with the Lomond hills of Fife behind. Standing here, I also have a wonderful vista of the whole sweep of the Firth of Forth—from the west, where it widens from the mouth of the river Forth to the east, where it joins the North Sea. To the west, just visible against the sky, the twin balletic leaps of the Forth Bridges (one rail, one road) connect the southern edge of the estuary with the northern. Where those bridges now span the gap, where the picturesque villages of North and South Queensferry can still be seen on either shore, Queen Margaret established hostels and ferries for pilgrims to the shrine of Saint Andrew on the north coast.

The view beyond the city—broad, low bands of pewter-colored sea and sky with undulating green between—can't have changed much since Margaret looked at it. Perhaps it was one of the last things she saw, on a day as wet and bleak as this; she died in the castle, probably very near where I now stand. The final years of Margaret's life must have been lonely ones: Lanfranc, her old Norman friend and ally, had died in 1089; Turgot had left to be prior of Durham two years before. Her health failed rapidly after the spring of 1093; she was not yet fifty but had worn out her body with fasting, and "lived her life hard," as Lucy Menzies has observed.[14] For the last six months of her life, she was seldom able to leave her bed. By November she was in constant pain and filled with forebodings about Malcolm, who was away, embroiled in what would be his last invasion of England. She knew her own death to be near, "but in her greatest paines, no complaint was heard to proceed from her innocent mouth."[15]

As Margaret lay dying, a cross clasped in her hands, her son Edgar came in with the news that her husband and their eldest son had been killed in the battle at Alnwick. At the same time—the news of the deaths of both king and heir having traveled fast among other claimants to the throne—the castle was already under attack by Malcolm's brother Donald Bane.

Margaret died as she had lived, deeply anchored in God, steadfast and quiet amid the din of war. "Her departure was so calm, so tranquil, that we may conclude her soul passed at once to the land of eternal rest and peace," Turgot tells us.[16]

Even as the castle was once more besieged, Margaret's body was shrouded in haste and carried in secret from her private chamber, through the west gate, and down the steep west face of the Castle Rock. Under cover of an Edinburgh *haar,* the thick white mist from the sea, her sons Ethelred and Edgar bore her body safely out of the battle, and home to the church she had built some twenty years before—by means of the ferry she had established for the ease of pilgrims. From where I stand in the drizzling rain outside the chapel, I can just see the place, upriver to the west, marked now by the two bridges that span the estuary.

On the other side of the bridges lies Dunfermline—once the religious and political capital of Scotland, the site of Margaret's first home in the north, where she built her first "new" church, where she and Malcolm were married. It is also where her body was buried—twice: first under the altar at her Church of the Holy Trinity in November 1093, and then, after her canonization in 1250, in a special shrine just to the east of the high altar. This reliquary chapel must have been beautiful to behold[17] and was famous throughout the Middle Ages; thousands of devout pilgrims made their way from all across Europe to pray there, hoping that the compassionate queen would intercede for the poor and needy in heaven as she once did at court. The chapel itself, however, was destroyed in the vandalizing days of civil war and Reformation. Only a stone plinth remains, inside an iron railing, to show where the exquisite medieval shrine once was.

In 1993, in recognition of the nine hundredth anniversary of Margaret's death in 1093, Historic Scotland and other agencies published leaflets and maps to mark the "Trail of Queen Margaret." Many of the places associated with Scotland's sainted queen were renovated or remembered. Not only Dunfermline's abbey, tower, and cave are memorials: as far south as the Borders, the famous abbeys of Jedburgh,

Kelso, and Melrose were all founded by King David I, Margaret's son. As far north as Angus, where Margaret built a chapel on an island in Forfar Loch, and as far west as Iona, Margaret's legacy is visible.

But a real sense of her spirit is elusive in many of these places—obstructed as the windows in her chapel were by the ignorance of other ages, other needs, sometimes obscured even by well-meaning attempts to celebrate her memory. At any rate, my own wanderings in search of Margaret seem to lead back to Edinburgh Castle, and to the tiny chapel at its highest point, seemingly carved by prayer itself out of the living rock.

It is here, in the small chapel at the heart of the castle stronghold, that, for this pilgrim at least, Saint Margaret, queen of Scotland, seems most real, most present. Maybe because this place, like her life, is built so firmly not only on the Castle Rock but also on the rock of her steadfast faith. The rain still hisses against the narrow windows; the peace continues deep and strong. The words of the psalmist come readily to mind here: "The LORD is my rock, my fortress, . . . my God, my rock in whom I take refuge, . . . my stronghold" (Ps. 18:2).

Canterbury Cathedral

Chapter 5

Canterbury Cathedral
& Thomas Becket

"I am ready to embrace death"

The Cathedral's East Chapel draws visitors past Becket's shrine
into a startlingly contemporary story of Christian martyrdom.

—DAVID

THE DAY IS OVERCAST. Rain has just passed over Canterbury. I have come from London via a train journey of ninety minutes; pilgrims in Chaucer's era would have taken weeks to walk the same distance.

I follow the bend of the city wall, past gardens of red-flowering horse chestnut trees, until the cathedral's bell tower comes into view. For a moment I experience what I felt so briefly on the train: a kindred sense of identity, albeit undeserved, with footsore pilgrims as they approached Canterbury's spires.

I arrive at the great West Door in time for evensong, and an usher leads me into the well-lit choir, a narrow, intimate setting between the vast nave and the main altar. A boys choir sings "O Clap Your Hands" by Ralph Vaughan Williams, accompanied by trumpet and organ that echo off the carved stone. A priest reads of Christ's promise to the disciples: "Lo, I am with you always."

Not far from where we worship, the archbishop of Canterbury, Thomas Becket, was murdered shortly before vespers on December 29,

1170. Four Norman knights, interpreting King Henry II's outburst— "Will no one rid me of this turbulent priest?"—as royal command, had hurried to Canterbury to demand that Becket recant ecclesial positions putting him at odds with the king.

As the knights arrived at the cathedral, they shouted, "Where is Thomas Becket, traitor to the king and the kingdom?" Becket had begun to climb steps into the north transept but came down the stairs to meet his assailants, replying, "Here I am, not traitor to the king, but a priest of God. What do you want of me?"

He could have saved himself, fleeing to the roof or acceding to the knights' demands; he had returned to England from safe exile in France only weeks before. But the archbishop instead faced his attackers, saying, "For the name of Jesus and the protection of the Church I am ready to embrace death."[1]

What gave Becket such resolve? I glance along the choir wall to the crucifix. Lest there be any doubt, his words—"Into thy hands, O Lord, I commend my spirit"—link Canterbury to Calvary. According to eyewitnesses, a sword blade sliced through his head with such force that the metal shattered as it struck the stone floor.

The martyrdom site itself, in the north transept near steps leading to the cloisters, seems startlingly unobtrusive. Becket, whose piety prompted him to wear a hair shirt and daily wash the feet of thirteen beggars, would no doubt have appreciated the inconspicuous location. His life as well as his death drew the faithful. Once the king's chancellor and then as archbishop the king's archadversary, Becket "had put off the Secular man," observed a twelfth-century monk, "and put on Jesus Christ."

In the wake of Becket's death and ensuing miracles attributed to his intercessions, Canterbury soon rivaled Rome and Santiago de Compostela as Europe's most famous pilgrimage destination. Over the years pilgrims traveled to Becket's shrine for many reasons, often in penance or thanksgiving, at times in search of healing. But the cathedral now beckons for a lesser-known reason. Not far from a medieval murder site, visitors enter into a story of contemporary Christian martyrdom.

The easternmost end of Canterbury Cathedral opens into a semi-circular chapel lit with high stained-glass windows. Known as the Corona Chapel (having once housed a portion of Becket's skull as a relic), the East Chapel now directs visitors' attention toward the more recently slain. A sign on the wall explains:

> Throughout the centuries men and women have given their lives for Christianity. Our own century is no exception. Their deaths are in union with the life-giving death of Our Lord Jesus Christ the Savior of mankind. In this Chapel we thank God for the sacrifice of martyrdom whereby truth is upheld and God's providence enriched. We pray that we may be worthy of their sacrifice.

On both sides of the East Chapel's entrance, two lecterns hold identical three-ring binders. Plastic-sheathed pages inside offer brief biographical sketches of more than a dozen twentieth-century martyrs, among them Martin Luther King Jr., Archbishop Oscar Romero of El Salvador, and the priest and hermit Charles de Foucauld, killed in the Sahara. Edith Stein and Maria Skobtsova are included, along with Dietrich Bonhoeffer and Maximilian Kolbe, as victims of Nazi concentration camps. Turning the pages, I come across unfamiliar names of priests killed in Russia, Iran, and Uganda.

Each biographical entry seems meager at best, the occasional photograph faded. Set beneath a vaulted edifice with glorious ornamentation, the slim binders of names are likely the flimsiest objects in the cathedral. Yet located so close to where Becket himself was killed, the list seems somehow to illumine all those who recognize a higher authority than Caesar's. Facing death, rather than escaping it, runs like a scarlet thread through the history of martyrdom. Refuge remains an option for many men and women; instead, like Canterbury's archbishop, they descend the stairs to face the swords. Without fanfare, in stained-glass stillness, the East Chapel transforms the beatitude—"Blessed are those who are persecuted"—into lives of flesh and spilled blood.

The cathedral designated its East Chapel "The Chapel of Saints and Martyrs of Our Own Time" after the murder of Anglican Archbishop Janani Luwum of Uganda by Idi Amin's forces in 1977.

"His [Archbishop Luwum's] killing had a great effect on us Anglicans," recalls British writer and former Canterbury Canon A. M. Allchin, who preached the Sunday following the assassination. "I felt a stronger sense of Thomas Becket than I ever had before because Janani Luwum was an Archbishop killed by a king. I felt the stones of Canterbury shuddered in sympathy."[2]

The cathedral chose to limit the names listed in the binder to only fifteen. "From time to time candidates are put forward, and we had to say, in effect, that we are not the agency for creating new saints," explains former Residentiary Canon Peter Brett. "We therefore curtailed the list and made it representative of all who are persecuted for their faith in our own day."[3] Standing in the East Chapel, some visitors for the first time understand martyrdom not as isolated acts in history but as a pattern in contemporary faith.

What would a complete martyrs' list look like? A recent one would tally individual stories of suffering countenanced by governments in Africa, Asia, and the Middle East, spotlighting countries that have made it a crime to convert to Christianity or to disseminate religious publications. With her book *In the Lion's Den,* Nina Shea, director of the Center for Religious Freedom at Freedom House, based in Washington, D.C., chronicles contemporary men and women "persecuted and martyred before an unknowing, indifferent world and a largely silent Christian community. . . . The atrocities include torture, enslavement, rape, imprisonment, forcible separation of children from parents, killings, and massacres."[4]

Few observers expect the persecution to diminish. "Evangelical and Catholic communities in the Third World are acutely vulnerable," writes human rights advocate Michael Horowitz, who adds that "the mounting persecution of Christians eerily parallels the persecution of Jews, my people, during much of Europe's history. Today, minority Christian communities have become chosen scapegoats in radical Islamic and remnant Communist regimes, where they are demonized and caricatured through populist campaigns of hate and terror."[5]

World Christian Trends A.D. 30–A.D. 2200, by David Barrett and Todd Johnson, provides an exhaustive, thirty-eight-page chronicle of the casualty toll from religious persecution, using a carefully crafted definition: "Christian martyrs are . . . believers in Christ who have lost their lives prematurely, in situations of *witness,* as a result of human hostility."

"Most Christians today think that persecution ended with Constantine," says Barrett. "Historically, the rate over the past 2000 years is that just under 1 percent of all Christians get murdered for their faith."[6] Barrett and Johnson calculate that the twentieth century saw more Christians killed—an estimated 45,400,000—for their faith than all preceding centuries combined.[7]

A band of tourists, hushed and reverent, walks toward the East Chapel from the Chapter House, which hosted the first performance of T. S. Eliot's play *Murder in the Cathedral* during the 1935 Canterbury Festival. The play probes Becket's motives with a cast not only of priests, chorus, and knights but also of tempters who, through lures of secular power and spiritual pride, sought to beguile the archbishop away from his rendezvous with martyrdom.

Writing during the rise of fascist dictatorships, Eliot "found that the basic conflict of the twentieth century came very near to repeating that of the twelfth."[8] Who are we in this play performed daily on the world's stage? For most of us, certainly not Becket with his hair shirt and morals. A servant who reportedly tried to stop the blows? The tempters perhaps? Surely not the knights?

With a chilling recognition it dawns on me: *We are the audience,* seated with folded hands, watching as across our field of vision people fall beneath the sword.

In *Murder in the Cathedral* Becket confronted tempters eager to lull him into passivity. Speaking from my own experience, bystanders to contemporary martyrdom face temptations of their own. For example, as I read again the East Chapel's list of names, I find my doubts spreading like clouds over their shining stories. Did they in fact die for their Christian faith? Wasn't Martin Luther King Jr. murdered because of racial rather than religious hatred? Did the Nazis condemn Edith Stein to Auschwitz as a nun or because she was born Jewish? And Charles de Foucauld: wasn't this Catholic monk, whose life inspired the Little Brothers of Jesus, shot by a Tuareg revolutionary who viewed him as a French colonialist?

As I glance about the cathedral, I am tempted for a moment to deny even Becket his martyrdom. Didn't his quarrel with King Henry II trace back less to religion than politics—to ecclesiastic privileges that threatened royal power? I notice that one of my guidebooks characterizes the archbishop as "querulous and legalistic," embracing martyrdom "with an . . . unseemly and even self-indulgent" enthusiasm, adding in a final swipe, "It is difficult not to sympathize with the king."[9]

David Barrett, however, provides perspective: "Look more at the motivation of the person giving his life, not the one taking it," he suggests. "I'm less worried about what a killer's motivation is—whether political or ethnic or not—than 'did the Christian get into the situation because he or she was a Christian?'"[10]

An even more subtle temptation masquerades as a laudable aversion to exclusivity. Reading of Christians bombed to death in the Sudan or churches burned in southern India, we can stifle our concern by noting that others are persecuted too. It is a vital point, for the list is indeed long and includes in recent years Sunni Muslims, Baha'is, Hasidic Jews, Tibetan Buddhists, and Sudanese animists. But in practice, such immediate extinguishing of any spotlight on Christians has left many fellow believers in the dark, oblivious to the suffering by people of any faith.

In his *Canterbury Tales,* Geoffrey Chaucer wrote:

. . . from every shires ende
Of Engelond to Caunterbury they wende,

The hooly blisful martir for to seke,
That hem hath holpen whan that they were seeke.[11]

Over the centuries, visitors to Canterbury have often unburdened themselves of various items before leaving the cathedral. Some relinquished treasure (when Erasmus came, he reported that gold, silver coins, and jewels covered Becket's shrine); other pilgrims, miraculously healed, left behind sickness or blindness.

Current visitors might honor Becket's sacrifice by leaving behind their indifference to those suffering for the sake of faith. Confronting his royal assassins, Canterbury's archbishop once proclaimed, "For the name of Jesus and the protection of the Church I am ready to embrace death."[12] For contemporary Christians to hear similar words—being uttered in languages around the world—would amount to a miracle in itself, a healing of deafness.

As I leave the cathedral, an elderly priest greets me companionably and asks where I am living in Britain. When he hears Scotland's St. Andrews, he murmurs, "Beautiful place," then shakes his head. "If only they'd been able to keep their cathedral."

I tell him that only the day before I'd been walking in its ruins—the remains of what was once the largest cathedral in Scotland, dismembered by Reformation politics, incendiary mobs, and North Sea gales—and had felt similar regret.

He shrugs. "You'll find much the same feeling here," he says, gesturing toward Canterbury's still-standing Gothic stone, "but a little livelier spirit."

The priest's regret recalls ancient frictions and sectarian violence. Its legacy cannot be avoided on St. Andrews's historic streets, given the initials of bonfire victims encobbled in the pavement. Protestant-Catholic strife still clouds Northern Ireland. From the Crusades to Kosovo, we are all too aware of Christians inflicting persecution.

But what Canterbury opens is a small window onto a landscape of Christians suffering persecution. The East Chapel draws pilgrims past Becket's biography, a single, safe story of the distant past, to glimpse a global story of astonishing proportion.

My room for the night is in a fourteenth-century pilgrims' inn, built adjacent to Christ Church Gate and the cathedral grounds. I have dinner at the inn, bent over brochures and books about Canterbury, and then return to my room for an early night. Through mullioned windows, the low-ceilinged room looks out on the cathedral itself, its soaring limestone brilliantly illuminated by spotlights.

It is a Thursday, the one night of the week when bell ringers practice. I can see, high in the lighted Oxford Tower, a company of men pulling steadily on ropes, filling the evening with sound. John Donne, dean of another English cathedral, once wrote of bells and what he called "the church universal": "Any man's death diminishes me, because I am involved in mankind, and therefore never send to know for whom the bell tolls; it tolls for thee."[13]

Sitting at a desk, I open the inn's window, letting fragrant spring air flood into the room. For a moment, the pealing of the bells becomes like a tally of lives given in faith, a tolling of arrests, tortures, and executions.

The comfortable inn creaks as guests return along its sloping floors to their rooms for the evening. It has been a long day, and I add an extra pillow to my bed.

Writing of the body of Christ, Paul told the Corinthians, "If one member suffers, all suffer together with it" (1 Cor. 12:26).

I pull back the sheets and turn out the light. A reflected glow from the cathedral illumines my room. As the ringing of bells dies away over Canterbury, I stretch out in the soft bed and fall asleep.

Julian's Shrine, Norwich

Chapter 6

Norwich and Lady Julian

"God at the center of everything"

Not only Lady Julian's anchor hold but also the magnificent nearby cathedral (centuries old even in Julian's lifetime) are places drenched in prayer. In the cathedral, be sure to look for the stained-glass window of Julian—and her legendary cat.

—Deborah

From the window of my room, upstairs at the All Hallows Convent guesthouse, I can see the neighboring parish church, silhouetted faintly against the night sky of Norwich. The church is dark, but I know the small bulwark of Mother Julian's shrine is on the side of the building facing me. It is a comforting thought as I draw the curtains and get ready for bed—almost as though Julian herself is just next door.

I have come to Norwich on pilgrimage to visit this church and shrine, anchor hold of the fourteenth-century mystic known only as Julian of Norwich, whose *Revelations of Divine Love* have disturbed, puzzled, and attracted me for years.

In May of 1373, when Julian was "thirty and a half years old," she tells us, she fell gravely ill and was close to death. A priest was called to administer the last rites. While she was in this state, gazing at a crucifix the priest held before her eyes, Julian experienced a series of sixteen visions, or "showings," of Christ on the cross. At some point shortly after her unexpected recovery, she wrote a brief account of her experience (now known as "the short text").

No one knows when she took up her life as an anchorite—a person dedicated to God and the church by means of a solitary life, although not necessarily in religious orders—but it seems that for some twenty years she prayed and meditated about these "showings" and eventually wrote what we know as "the long text" of her book.

Although Julian claims to have been unlettered at the time she received her "showings," her book is in fact a marvel. Not only does it have such rhetorical skill and literary merit as to warrant comparison with her contemporary, Geoffrey Chaucer, but also it is richly steeped in the Latin Vulgate scriptures, solid trinitarian theology, and the foundational monastic writings of Western Christianity. Hers is the first book known to have been written by a woman in English. After centuries of obscurity, it is now regarded as a spiritual classic—one so particularly suited to contemporary needs that one scholar has even suggested that "in some mysterious providence of God her wisdom has been 'saved up' for our generation."[1]

Of all the great medieval women mystics, no one is more luminously certain than Julian of the reality and goodness of God—while simultaneously more deeply aware of the sinfulness of the human heart and the suffering inherent in human life. All we can do, she knows, is "seek, suffer and trust."[2]

But the God we seek and trust in the midst of our suffering loves us more than we can imagine: "There is no created being who can know how much and how sweetly and how tenderly the Creator loves us."[3] God is "endless delight"[4]; God makes and loves and keeps all that is.[5] God is at the center of all things[6]—the inner meaning of everything. When she prayed to know the meaning of the "showings" given to her, Julian received this answer: "What, do you wish to know your Lord's meaning in this thing? Know it well, love was his meaning. Who reveals it to you? Love. What did he reveal to you? Love. Why does he reveal it to you? For love."[7]

Tantalizingly little is known of Julian, including her Christian name; Julian may be only the name she took from the church of St. Julian (probably Saint Julian of Antioch, a fourth-century martyr), where she lived as an anchorite in a cell built against the outside wall of the church. The typical construction of such medieval anchor holds (as assumed by the *Ancrene Riwle,* an anonymous twelfth-century manual for anchorites, upon which Julian evidently established the pattern of her life) allowed for a window opening onto the nave of the church, through which she could observe Mass and receive Holy Communion. The cell would also have had a window on the outside wall, not only to admit light and air but also to permit Julian to see and hear the people who came for counsel.

I have always loved the image of a contemplative life as one lived with a window on the church and a window on the world. I suspect I had, before I came to Norwich, a romantic notion of myself sitting in imaginary conversation with Julian at her "outside" window (where Margery Kempe[8] consulted her)—or kneeling at her inside window, gazing at the altar as Julian must have done.

I was disappointed, then, to learn that the present shrine—a lovely side chapel in the church, with a simple plaque and authentic-looking wooden doors set in Norman stonework—is a reconstruction of Julian's original cell. In fact it is a reconstruction adjoining a reconstruction—the original cell was demolished in the Reformation, and the church itself was almost completely destroyed by a bomb in World War II. Both church and shrine have been lovingly rebuilt on the original site (two fragments of the original foundation can still be seen in the shrine)—but I couldn't help regretting the lost opportunity to touch with my own hands the seven-hundred-year-old stones hallowed by Julian's faithfulness.

I was also disappointed to realize that so little can be known of Julian's life or how she wrote her book. No one, even here in Norwich, can tell me where she was born; when she died; who taught her to read, write, think, and pray; if she ever married and had children; or where she is buried. Oddly, for a while, I feel her living reality recede rather than approach in this place she lived so long ago.

Once again, as so often happens on our journeys of faith, I had to stop and readjust my purposes, consider again why I was here. I remembered T. S. Eliot's insight in "Little Gidding":

. . . what you thought you came for
Is only a shell, a husk of meaning
From which the purpose breaks. . . .
. . . .
You are not here to verify,
Instruct yourself, or inform curiosity
Or carry report. You are here to kneel
Where prayer has been valid.[9]

The actual stones on which Julian knelt are gone. But I can still let the real purpose break through the husk of my intention. I can kneel where prayer—hers and thousands of others'—has been valid.

And kneel I do. The air in the church is so cold that our breath hangs in clouds before our faces as we pray the responses at Holy Communion that November morning. Aside from the priest, there are only half a dozen habited Anglican nuns and me at the Eucharist, which we celebrate in Julian's shrine. Even so small a congregation nicely fills the tiny space.

Behind the altar an unusual stained-glass window commemorates Julian; I linger after the service to look at it more closely. The scene depicted on the window, a woman kneeling at the foot of the cross, seems at first glance to be merely conventionally appropriate for Julian, whose visions were given in response to her prayer for a truer understanding of the Passion, in the context and presence of Christ crucified.

However, a closer look at the window reveals that, although Jesus bears the marks of the nails on his hands and feet and wears the crown of thorns, he is supported not by the wooden beams of the cross but by the twining leaves and flowers of a great sheaf of lilies. Moreover, his upraised arms and crossed feet give the impression not of agony but almost of dancing—and he is smiling as he looks down at the woman. Clearly this is Christ crucified but also somehow Christ risen.

The image is an excellent illustration of Julian's conviction of the

supreme friendship of our courteous Lord. . . . [who] shows himself to the soul, happily and with the gladdest countenance, welcoming it as a friend, as if it had been in pain and in prison, saying: My dear darling, I am glad that you have come to me in all your woe. I have always been with you, and now you see me loving, and we are made one in bliss.[10]

Inscribed in the glass panes over the woman's head is perhaps Julian's most famous line—echoed by T. S. Eliot in "Little Gidding" at the end of *Four Quartets*—"All shall be well." At first sight, again, this is an odd assertion to accompany the Passion, and an odd one to hear from fourteenth-century Norwich—which lost an estimated half of its population to the bubonic plague in three separate outbreaks. Julian received her visions four years after the third outbreak of the plague in Norwich in 1369, in the midst of an unspecified nearly fatal illness of her own. Clearly her assurance that "all shall be well, and all shall be well, and all manner of thing shall be well"[11] was no facile optimism but the ringing assurance of a soul that had found its center, and the eternal love of God at the center of that.

~

Julian expresses her conviction of this mystery of God's constant love in some bold—even startling—ways. Troubling to some (and misunderstood by many) is her insistence that there is no wrath in God.

> I saw truly that our Lord was never angry, and never will be. Because he is God, he is good, he is truth, he is love, he is peace; and his power, his wisdom, his charity and his unity do not allow him to be angry. . . . God is that goodness which cannot be angry, for God is nothing but goodness.[12]

There is plenty of anger, Julian readily admits, mixed up in our sinfulness—but it is on our side, not God's. All the upheaval and change in our spiritual condition occurs in us, not in God.

> For anger is no more than a perversity and striving against peace and love.
> And it is caused either by lack of strength, or lack of wisdom, or lack of goodness. This lack is not found in God, but in us. . . .
> For this was a high marvel to the soul and it was shown continually in all the Showings, and I looked on it carefully: it was shown that, of his nature, our Lord cannot forgive, for he cannot be angry. It would be impossible.[13]

This is startling theology indeed, and may seem at first to be not only glib and indulgent but contrary to much traditional Christian teaching and scriptural witness.

Julian herself did not take this "showing" lightly. She wrestled with the idea that there is no wrath in God. "How can this be?" she asks.

> For I know by the ordinary teaching of Holy Church and by my own feeling that the blame of our sins continually hangs upon us. . . .
>   I could have no patience because of great fear and perplexity. . . .
>   I cried within me with all my might, beseeching God for help.[14]

Julian perseveres with great courage and integrity and concludes—reassured by Jesus from the cross—that the startling revelation that there is no wrath in God is deeply true. However, she—ever a faithful daughter of the church—stops far short of urging a view of God that would tend toward an easy tolerance of sin.

Furthermore, a careful reading of Julian makes it clear that she is at pains only to remain faithful to her own visions, which occurred while she was in a state of grace and longing only for a truer understanding of her Lord's suffering and love. She is not speculating on what might otherwise obtain: "The revelation was shown to reveal goodness, and little mention was made in it of evil."[15] Nevertheless, she does see that God "opposes [those] who in malice and malignity work to frustrate and oppose God's will."[16]

However, for those "who would be saved"[17]—who, like Julian, are not aligned with malignity but helplessly struggle and fall—there is no anger at all. God looks on our struggling and falling "with pity and not with blame; for this passing life does not require us to live wholly without sin. He loves us endlessly, and we sin customarily, and he reveals it to us most gently."[18] "Our courteous Lord does not want his servants to despair because they fall often and grievously; for our falling does not hinder him in loving us."[19]

It is not that God does not mind our sinning. It is—and this is so hard for us to believe!—simply that, in truth, nothing can ever separate us from God's love, which never falters, never changes, never ends. No amount of grim striving after perfection in this life can save us—

nor does shame or punishment benefit us. We can in fact do nothing at all to save ourselves except rejoice that God is doing so.

> And this was the highest joy that the soul understood, that God himself will do it, and I shall do nothing at all but sin.[20]

> Only pain blames and punishes, and our courteous Lord comforts and succours. . . .
> And the loving regard which he kept constantly on his servant, and especially when he fell, it seemed to me that it could melt our hearts for love and break them in two for joy.[21]

The vision of God's inherent lack of anger toward us, no matter how often or grievously we fall into sin, achieves its greatest clarity and resonance in the context of another of Julian's famous and startling revelations, that of the motherhood of God: "As truly as God is our Father," Julian insists, "so truly is God our Mother."[22]

Characteristically, Julian gathers whole handfuls of relational names for God (Father, Mother, Brother, Spouse, Nurse) to describe the richness of the ways God loves us, and she seems at times to be speaking of any or all the Persons of the Trinity as meeting us in any or all of these intimacies. However, she returns over and over to the central reality of Christ our Mother: "All the lovely works and all the sweet loving offices of beloved motherhood are appropriated to the second person [of the Trinity]. . . . Our saviour is our true Mother, in whom we are endlessly born and out of whom we shall never come."[23]

Julian delights in the image of Christ as our Mother—the One who carries us, who brings us to life, who nurtures and protects and tenderly loves us. But it is especially important that we know Christ as our Mother when we sin:

> Often when our falling and our wretchedness are shown to us, we are so much afraid and so greatly ashamed of ourselves that we scarcely know where we can put ourselves. But then our courteous Mother does not wish us to flee away, for nothing would be less pleasing to him; but he then wants us to behave like a child. For when it is distressed and frightened,

it runs quickly to its mother; and if it can do no more, it calls to the mother for help with all its might. So he wants us to act as a meek child, saying: My kind Mother, my gracious Mother, my beloved Mother, have mercy on me. I have made myself filthy and unlike you, and I may not and cannot make it right except with your help and grace.[24]

The primary way that our "precious Mother Jesus" sustains and helps us is by feeding us. Julian's sense of this is characteristically direct: "The mother can give her child to suck of her milk, but our precious Mother Jesus can feed us with himself, and does, most courteously and most tenderly, with the blessed sacrament, which is the precious food of true life."[25]

During the Middle Ages—in fact, from at least the fifth century on—a central image in Christian art and symbol for the sacrificial love of Christ, especially as manifest in the sacrament of the Eucharist, was a maternal one: a mother pelican, who was thought to feed her young with blood from her own breast.

Julian stops short of using the pelican metaphor, but I carry this image with me as I leave the church and walk (on the lookout for pelicans among the river birds that wheel overhead) through the narrow cobbled streets to Norwich Cathedral in the center of town. The cathedral, where people have worshiped God since its consecration in 1101, is a glorious, soaring affair of honey-colored stone and ancient peace. In the choir I discover an unusual fourteenth-century bronze lectern, shaped not as the traditional eagle but, I rejoice to see, as a pelican, its bill to its breast.

~~

Between the cathedral and the parish church of St. Julian is the tiny home of Robert Llewelyn, Anglican priest, Julian scholar, and for many years the chaplain of the Julian shrine. I have written to ask if I might see him while I am in Norwich, and he has invited me to lunch. I am nervous as I knock on the front door—but his beaming face under snow-white hair and his open-armed welcome put me at ease at once. Over ham and tomato sandwiches and strong tea, we talk about Julian and her continuing ministry to pilgrims centuries after her death.

I mention my regret about the loss of the original church and cell. Smiling, he suggests it was perhaps not random loss so much as sacrifice: during World War II, the parish church was surrounded by tenements in an overcrowded part of the city, as it probably was in Julian's day. The church building in its tiny churchyard was the only open space in the area; it took a direct hit in the bombing. "It saved hundreds of lives," he tells me. "Even ten yards either way, and the loss of life would have been enormous. But the church was empty, and no one died when that bomb fell. Don't you imagine Julian would have wanted it that way?"

Once again I kneel where prayer has been valid, on the cold stone floor of Julian's cell. I am alone on this November morning, having stayed for solitary prayer of my own after the service. A wisp of incense lingers on the morning air; the taste of bread and wine is still in my mouth.

The fact that the shrine of Julian of Norwich is a reconstruction adjoining a reconstruction suddenly matters not at all.

The peace is as deep as the silence, and the silence feels companionable. I know somehow that not only is God present with me in this place, but Julian is as well. I can almost hear her voice, resonant with living trust in the love at the heart of all things:

> God revealed all this most blessedly, as though to say: See, I am God. See, I am in all things. See, I do all things. See, I never remove my hands from my works, nor ever shall without end. See, I guide all things to the end that I ordain them for, before time began, with the same power and wisdom and love with which I made them; how should anything be amiss?[26]

Securely anchored—at least for a moment—in Julian's conviction that indeed "all shall be well, and all shall be well, and all manner of thing shall be well," I rise from my knees and head for home.

Door knocker, Bemerton Church

Chapter 7

Bemerton and George Herbert

"Thy power and love, my love and trust"

It is almost worth hoping that the tiny church is locked when you arrive, for the great and awesome privilege of taking the massive old key in your own hands and opening the door—as Herbert himself opened it at least twice every day until his death.

—DEBORAH

I T HAS TAKEN me the better part of an hour to walk the two miles from the cathedral town of Salisbury to Bemerton, once a sleepy village, now a busy suburb, the once dusty lane now a noisy highway. I have dodged buses, breathed exhaust, been flattened against hedges and walls in the wake of hurtling trucks. I am rattled and weary and afraid I am lost.

And then suddenly I see it, unmistakably, just ahead: a tiny stone church, rooted calmly on its own peninsula amid the snarling traffic like a lighthouse on a rocky point standing fast against the sea.

Saint Andrew's Church, Bemerton: here it has stood for some six hundred years. Within the belfry sleeps the same bell that, every day for three brief but shining years nearly four centuries ago, the Anglican priest and poet George Herbert rang to call the faithful to morning and evening prayers. The south door, flanked by sentinel yew trees, protected from the weather by a low porch, is the one he opened.

Using both hands to lift down the key—so massive, so palpably ancient, that it could well be the same one George Herbert himself used—I unlock that heavy oak door myself and push it open before me. The church is empty, silent—the two-foot-thick walls effectively exclude the clamor of traffic—but the emptiness is resonant, the silence alive. It feels as though a bell has only just stopped ringing.

Instinctively I face the east end of the church, and—the place being so small—in the same moment I am standing before the altar, the same altar before which, after his induction as rector and alone in the church after the service, Herbert lay prostrate to vow fidelity and service to his Lord. There would not have been much room for the new rector to lie before the altar, I realize. Perhaps that is why, these hundreds of years later, the small space still seems filled with his gesture.[1]

Herbert's gesture has spoken to generations of Christians ever since—the gift of a life before the altar, given back to the One who gave it, an embodiment of passionate self-oblation and radical humility. In my undergraduate English major days, fed on Izaac Walton and Victorian sentimentality about the seventeenth century, I saw Herbert's prostration in Bemerton Church—in fact his whole life as a country priest—as an uncomplicated sacrifice of political and ecclesiastical ambition on the altar of rural obscurity, the outward sign of his inward choice "rather to serve at God's Altar, than to seek the honor of State employments."[2] Seen from the perspective of the tumultuous 1960s, Herbert appeared to me something of a social revolutionary (rather along the lines of a young Saint Francis of Assisi, dramatically stripping himself of his father's rich clothes and worldly expectations), renouncing power and privilege for a life of prayer and service to God's beloved poor.

More careful reading of Herbert's poems and his biographies has changed my undergraduate sense of what Herbert was really doing in that moment before the Bemerton altar. But far from diminishing their value, a closer look has made Herbert's poems and his "hidden" life even more meaningful—and far more helpful to my own life in God.

Rather than seeing his life as a disillusioned renunciation of the world's temptations to power, I have come to see it as a courageous acceptance, marked by much struggle, of the will of God for him in his weakness. Not the right use of power in the world or the church, nor the dangers of power to a holy life, but utter trust in God's love whatever the external circumstances was ultimately the issue for Herbert. Our business as Christians is not control but trust:

> Whether I fly with angels, fall with dust,
> Thy hands made both, and I am there:
> Thy power and love, my love and trust
> Make one place ev'rywhere.[3]

I kneel at the Communion rail on a needlepoint cushion worked with *GH* (the initials accompanied by a lute, pen, and tree, all within the embrace of a cross) and thank God for the grace of Herbert's life and work, letting my mind wander over the events that led him (and thereby me) to this obscure village in south Wiltshire, England.

George Herbert was born in 1593, the seventh of ten children, into a large and distinguished family, in the county of Montgomery on the Welsh border. His ancestors and kinsmen were earls of Pembroke and knights of Shropshire; his remarkable mother, Magdalene, was a close friend of the Anglican poet John Donne. The Herberts ranked among the highest in the land, accustomed to power, privilege, and public service.

George Herbert's early life was entirely in keeping with these traditions, although he was both more devout in faith and less robust in health than his siblings. He received his master's degree at Trinity College, Cambridge, at the age of twenty and soon after was made a fellow, despite the frequent "fevers, and other infirmities"[4] that were to plague him all his life. Appointed to the prestigious office of public orator for the university, he successfully stood for Parliament in 1624. At the age of thirty-one, he seemed launched upon a conventionally illustrious public life.

But suddenly that trajectory changed. Within a month of the dissolution of the Parliament of 1624, Herbert had obtained leave of his duties as public orator at Cambridge and moved so swiftly toward ordination as a deacon in the Church of England as to require a special dispensation from the archbishop of Canterbury.

Scholars have debated for decades what led Herbert to turn his back on life at court and seek holy orders instead. Herbert's first biographer, Izaak Walton, attributes the abrupt *volte face* to the deaths of his friends and patrons: the duke of Richmond, the marquis of Hamilton, and King James.[5]

English professor and Episcopal priest John N. Wall Jr. suggests, however, that Herbert's swift departure from public life was due not to a failure of patronage or to thwarted personal ambition but to disillusionment with the notion—so dear to the hearts of many seventeenth-century Anglicans—of achieving social transformation through political change:

> Herbert's idealistic visions of insuring the peace through service to the crown were dashed by the warmongering of Prince Charles in the Parliament of 1624. . . . To hold to one's idealism in the face of such realities could for Herbert be achieved only by returning to the source of that idealism, the Church . . . a return not so much to earlier hopes of ecclesiastical employment, but to the life of the Christian community, marked in Stuart England by devotion to the round of prayer and Bible reading embodied in the services of Morning and Evening Prayer.[6]

Whatever the specific reasons, clearly something led Herbert to reject illustrious political careers not only at Cambridge and at court, but also—courteously refusing the example of John Donne, dean of Saint Paul's Cathedral—power and prestige within the church. Against the advice of his friends, who tried to persuade him that burying himself in a rural parish was "too mean an employment, and too much below his birth, and the excellent abilities and endowments of his mind,"[7] Herbert moved steadily away from the halls of power and in 1630 was inducted as rector of Saint Andrew's, Bemerton. As Nicholas Ferrar of Little Gidding famously put it: "Quitting . . . all the opportunities that he had for worldly preferment, he [Herbert] betook himself to the Sanctuary and Temple of God, choosing rather to serve at God's Altar, than to seek the honor of State employments."[8]

Thus did the long road lead to the altar of Bemerton Church, and to the poetry so justly celebrated for its luminous trust and joy in God. In a less bellicose and fractured political climate, perhaps George

Herbert would have become a wise and conscientious high-ranking government official, and neither he nor I would ever have knelt in Bemerton Church.

⌁

Once Herbert had prayerfully decided that neither political power nor ecclesial prominence but humble service was the key to a holy life, it might seem that Herbert's famous "spiritual conflicts" were at an end, and all would fade into the bucolic peace of the English countryside at twilight. And indeed Herbert's life has often been interpreted just that way. However, as T. S. Eliot has pointed out, "to think of Herbert as the poet of a placid and comfortable easy piety is to misunderstand utterly the man and his poems."[9]

In fact the renouncing of his "Court hopes" in order to seek to serve God as a country priest was neither the end of the story nor even the definitive vocational choice. Herbert did not want just political power; at a different level, he also simply wanted the ordinary sort of personal freedom and public usefulness that people of goodwill, in good health and spirits, take for granted. But even this sort of "power" was denied Herbert, who was captive to illness and depression for most of his life, and suffered terribly from a conviction of his own uselessness.

More poignant to me by far than Herbert's desire for "place and power" are his simple longings to be of any use to anyone, and to give something back to God, who had done so much for him. More pervasive in his poems than the struggle against the world's temptations is Herbert's struggle against melancholy. In the autobiographical poem "Affliction (I)," he protests that sickness and sorrow[10] have rendered him helpless and ineffectual: "a blunted knife was of more use than I."[11] In the same poem, he confesses to God his bewilderment and fear for the future:

> . . . what thou wilt do with me
> None of my books will show:
> I read, and sigh, and wish I were a tree;
> For sure then I should grow

To fruit or shade: at least some bird would trust
Her household to me. . . .[12]

This sad restlessness, born of his felt inability to do anything for
the God who had done so much for him, runs through much of
Herbert's life and poetry. Even after taking holy orders and leaving behind Parliament and court, for a long time he found no peace. "I am
in all a weak disabled thing," he laments in "The Cross":

To have my aim, and yet to be
Further from it than when I bent my bow;
To make my hopes my torture, and the fee
Of all my woes another woe
Is . . . ev'n in Paradise to be a weed.[13]

Nevertheless, remembering that Christ also experienced the pain
of apparent failure yet trusted in God, Herbert ends the poem with the
words *Thy will be done.* Again, submission to the will of God in "love
and trust" provides the only resolution, the only way to peace.

Over and over again, this pattern of constriction and rebellion—
ending at last in "love and trust"—is the pattern of Herbert's poems.
This dynamic is not one of grudging or defeated surrender to a superior force, but a sense of being found, claimed, and healed by the restoration of an intimate relationship. Indeed, on his deathbed, in consigning
the "little book" of his poems to his friend Nicholas Ferrar, Herbert
called it "a picture of the many spiritual conflicts that have past betwixt
God and my soul, before I could subject mine to the will of Jesus my
master: in whose service I have now found perfect freedom."[14]

Increasingly Herbert seems to have discovered himself to be val-
ued by God not in terms of his usefulness (much less his "place and
power"[15]) but solely on the basis of that mystical parent-child relationship. "Not the decrees of power, but bands of love"[16] were ultimately
what held him fast.

⌒

In a paradox richly explored in his poetry, Herbert found the social usefulness and spiritual peace he had so long sought, not in public office

but in virtual invisibility: "My Life Is Hid in Him That Is My Treasure," he declared, quoting scripture—and literally hiding the text diagonally within the body of the poem.[17]

Herbert did, at the end of his life, deeply experience that "in [God's] will is our peace."[18] "The Flower," for example, brims with grateful wonder at the renewing power of grace:

How fresh, Oh Lord, how sweet and clean
Are thy returns! . . .

. . . .

Who would have thought my shrivel'd heart
Could have recover'd greenness? . . .

. . . .

And now in age I bud again,
After so many deaths I live and write;
I once more smell the dew and rain,
And relish versing: Oh my only light,
It cannot be
That I am he
On whom thy tempests fell all night.[19]

The brevity of George Herbert's tenure at Bemerton is poignant. He died at home in the rectory just across from the church, of tuberculosis, just before his fortieth birthday in 1633—only three years after his induction. But those three years were a lifetime in the making, and their light still shines. His poems, indisputably among the finest ever written in English, assure Herbert's legacy. Moreover, his devotional classic in prose, *The Country Parson,* written "that I may have a Mark to aim at,"[20] is "in its common sense and goodness," as Ronald Blythe has observed, "in the great tradition of guides to the pastoral vocation."[21]

Perhaps most valuable, Herbert has left "a Mark to aim at" for all of us who, like him, long to transcend a struggle for power in the church or in the world to find ourselves "hid in God who is our treasure."

Even centuries after his death, George Herbert still faces the altar in Bemerton Church. As I rise from my knees at the Communion rail (companionably near his memorial stone in the north wall), I turn around and notice the west window, which is a full-length portrait of Herbert in glass, meditatively standing with a lute tucked under his arm, next to a window commemorating Nicholas Ferrar of Little Gidding. Even on this grey afternoon in early fall, the window is luminous, the colors jewel-like—a fitting image for Herbert's hard-won, prayer-soaked peacefulness about his own "place and power" in the church and in the world.

Just as he found his vocation not in public office but in "hidden-ness," so Herbert admired the hiddenness of windows, which best ful-fill the ends for which they were created the more transparent they are. The "place and power" of a window, its whole usefulness and effec-tiveness, depend entirely on its ability to be firmly placed and then sim-ply to disappear and let the light shine through it. This village church, with its seasonal round of prayer and its close links with the daily lives of local people, was for Herbert a "glorious and transcendent place" where he hoped only "to be a window, through [God's] grace."[21]

To the right of the window, the rope for the church bell sweeps in a graceful curve from the belfry overhead. I run my hand lightly along the looped rope, which swings delicately in response.

The silence I had noticed upon entering is still alive, as though the bell had just been rung. I long for a way to take this ringing silence with me when I go—to carry away, like a pilgrim's blessing, the peace of the ancient, unheard bell.

I am reluctant to leave; the church breathes a nourishing peaceful-ness, speaks of the "sustaining power"[22] of God, and is remarkably redo-lent of Herbert's joyful trust. But this country parish was George Herbert's own place of struggle and repose; I must find another. I bow toward the altar and prepare to leave, prayerfully resolved to continue seeking my own "transcendent place, To be a window"—to listen, always, with God's help and Herbert's poetry, for "Church-bells beyond the stars heard."[23]

Atop the city wall, York

Chapter 8

York and Margaret Clitherow
& Mary Ward

"Hearts set on the pilgrim way"

The best way to see York is from the top of the old city wall. Try to walk at least part of the way if you get there at all, imagining all the people who have gone before you.

—DEBORAH

*I*T IS EXHILARATING to walk atop the city walls of York—especially on an April morning, with the sun flashing on the river Ouse and the wind scattering apple blossoms before me like confetti. I revel in knowing that I am, through the soles of my shoes, in direct contact with (my guidebook assures me) one of the finest surviving examples of medieval fortification in Europe, looking down on a thriving city that remembers not only the Middle Ages but also the Vikings, the Saxons, and the Romans. The massive wall is itself both rampart and road—protecting the city from its foes and providing a walkway for its citizens to follow. These twin qualities, of standing fast and moving forward, are also exemplified by two extraordinary women of York, Mary Ward (1585–1645) and Margaret Clitherow (1553–86). It is because of them that I am here.

From my vantage point atop the encircling wall, at the ancient gate of the Micklegate Bar, I can see, just on the far side, the decorous brick facade of the Bar Convent. This house was established in 1686 by the followers of Mary Ward, who during her lifetime was both praised as "a great servant of God" and condemned as a "heretic, schismatic, and rebel," and who is honored today as a heroic visionary, a pioneer of unenclosed religious life for women.

For thirty years this intrepid woman traveled tirelessly across Europe, founding schools for Catholic girls and laboring to establish a rule of life for women based on the Rule and Constitutions of the Society of Jesus. The Jesuits were themselves at that time a new and controversial order of priests, their life based not on medieval monastic norms of stability and long hours in chapel singing the divine office, but on freedom and mobility: being ready to go, in obedience, to the ends of the earth at a moment's notice "for the greater glory of God."[1] This was a revolutionary idea for men in vowed religious life; it was unheard-of for women. Furthermore, England had seen no convents of any kind for seventy years, since the dissolution of the monasteries by Henry VIII; young Catholic girls in Tudor England who felt called to cloistered life had to accept lifelong exile in Catholic Flanders or France. Nevertheless, Mary Ward knew from the age of fifteen that she had been called by God to religious life—not to conventional enclosure in a convent, but to a life of action inspired by the love of God and modeled on the example of the Jesuits.

Serenely undeterred by ferocious opposition to her dream and aware that only papal approval would secure the future of the congregation she envisioned (the Institute of the Blessed Virgin Mary, as it was eventually to be known[2]), Mary crossed the Alps four times, in winter, on foot, to present her case to the pope in person. She established schools for girls and Institute houses in England, France, Italy, Germany, Hungary, and the Low Countries. Her schools were much admired, but the radical notion of nonenclosure for women drew much opposition. Mary, however, was adamant: "I will not accept as much as two crossed sticks in the way of enclosure," she stoutly declared.[3]

She faced hostility not only from within the Catholic Church but from the Anglican establishment as well. She was so ardent and effective a Catholic in Elizabethan England, where Catholics were hunted as spies and executed as traitors, that the archbishop of Canterbury declared in frustration that she had "done more harm [to the Protestant cause] than many priests."[4] Imprisoned both by order of the Inquisition[5] and by the Protestant authorities, she lived to see her beloved Institute suppressed and dissolved by order of the pope, her schools closed, her life's work shattered. Yet Mary Ward remained steadfast in hope and peaceful to the end, urging her companions with characteristic "imperturbable gaiety"[6] to "be merry and doubt not our Master."[7] Today the Institute of the Blessed Virgin Mary, which continues as a vibrant teaching order, numbers several thousand members in five continents. The third oldest house is the Bar Convent here in York (the oldest living convent in England).

From its founding, the Bar Convent provided secret Masses for the Catholic community of York, as well as covert schooling for its daughters. In 1765, when the convent was rebuilt, it was still illegal to build a Catholic church in England;[8] to this day, the convent's magnificent chapel is completely hidden at the center of the house, invisible from the outside. A pitched roof conceals the sunken dome, and a hiding place for the priest was included as a matter of course: it was discovered about fifty years ago, when electrical wiring was being installed. The elegant Georgian brick building still presents a courteously bland face to the world, protecting the secret chapel at its heart, bearing architectural witness to a long era of persecution—and of standing fast.

Severe anti-Catholic decrees, born of Henry VIII's and Elizabeth I's insistence on being recognized as the sole heads of the church in England, made it illegal even to attend Mass. Those Catholics (called "recusants," meaning "refusers") who chose fidelity to Rome over obedience to the Tudors needed great courage. The illicit practice of the Catholic faith, especially the indispensable sacrament of the Mass, required clandestine gatherings with priests. These priests—often Jesuits—had been educated and ordained overseas, smuggled into England, and secretly passed from house to house to celebrate their forbidden

Masses. This was an act of treason, punishable by death, not only for the priests but also for the families that sheltered them.[9]

The valor of these recusants, determined to remain faithful Catholics whatever the consequences, is still striking today. Young Robert Coulton, challenged by the Protestant authorities, spoke for many when he said: "I hear say that England hath been a Catholic Christian country a thousand years afore this queen's reign and her father's. If that were the old highway to heaven, then why should I forsake it?"[10] Those who remained committed to "the old highway" paid dearly for that allegiance: recusants were stripped of land and title, forced to pay heavy fines, and sometimes spent years in prison for the privilege of nonattendance at Anglican worship.

Others paid for steadfast commitment to "the old highway" with their lives: during Elizabeth's reign, more than a hundred Roman Catholic priests were hunted down, imprisoned, tortured, and hanged as traitors, joined by sixty-two courageous laywomen and men. First among these was another valiant Yorkshire woman, Saint Margaret Clitherow, who is revered by Catholics around the world today as one of the Forty Martyrs of England and Wales.

Continuing my walk along the city wall, I come to the Lendal Bridge where it spans the broad Ouse. From the bridge, looking east inside the wall's embrace—and looking back in time a generation before Mary Ward—I can see the medieval Guildhall, where Margaret Clitherow was sentenced to death for harboring priests and hearing Mass in her home. Just down the river, at the next bridge, is the unmarked site of her execution.

These two remarkable women never met—Margaret died in 1586, at the age of thirty-three, when Mary was just one year old—but their lives connected in deep places, rooted in realities and allegiances that continued to sustain the faithful who came after them. The steadfast love of God and confidence in God's purposes that illumined both their lives shine across the centuries like the rhythmic signal of a lighthouse. Both their hearts were firmly "set upon the pilgrims' way."[11]

Margaret Clitherow was born around 1553, the year of the Catholic Queen Mary's accession, so in all probability she was baptized as a Catholic in her infancy and brought up as a Catholic until she was eight, when her widowed mother married a Protestant. After that—Queen Mary having died and Queen Elizabeth having ascended the throne—the religious influences in Margaret's growing-up years were all Protestant. At the age of fifteen she married John Clitherow,[12] a local widower and Protestant butcher old enough to be her father. Within three years of her marriage, however, Margaret had been reconciled to the Catholic Church, although we cannot know how or why. By the time she was a young matron of eighteen, her house was established as the principal Mass center—and thus the heart of the underground Catholic community—in York.[13]

For the rest of her life, Margaret befriended and harbored priests in her home, running a small (and highly illegal) school for the Catholic education of children, and "providing place and all things convenient" for celebration of the Mass. For most of a decade she was in and out of prison for these crimes, released once only long enough to deliver a child. Margaret's time in prison, in company with other recusant Catholics, seems to have been a profound experience of religious community: she used the time to study, pray, and strengthen her faith. During one of her long captivities, she learned to read and write.

But the deadly risks of recusancy caught up with her at last. A raid on the Clitherow house in March 1586 revealed the existence of the priest's hiding place in the attic (although the priest had time to escape), as well as the altar, chalice, books, and vestments for the Mass. Margaret was arrested, imprisoned, and formally charged. Allowed no counsel, she conducted her own defense, repeatedly refusing to consent to a trial ("Having made no offense, I need no trial," she calmly told the judge), lest her own and others' children be compelled to give testimony against her.

This compassionate and courageous stand doubtless saved several lives but cost Margaret her own: her refusal to enter a plea left the court no alternative under law but to pronounce the sentence of death by *peine forte et dure,* being pressed to death by heavy weights laid upon her prostrate body. This terrible death had been known to take as long as three days but was swift in Margaret's case: as the weights were laid on her, she prayed, "Jesu, Jesu, have mercy on me." Within a quarter of an hour she was dead.

The story of Margaret Clitherow is one Mary Ward would have heard from her cradle. The whole audacious enterprise of harboring fugitive priests was "very much a woman's affair"[14]—and shaped the heart of every household in which Mary lived as a child. The underground Catholic community in England in those days was essentially a matriarchy. As Father John Mush, one of the priests befriended by Margaret Clitherow, himself put it, "The gentlemen hereabouts have fallen away from the priests but the gentlewomen stood steadfastly to them."[15]

I suspect that Mary Ward was influenced in her vision of the Institute not only by the Jesuits but also by the "women and specifically wives"[16] who sheltered and assisted the priests, educated the children, prepared candidates for baptism, in fact shaped and nurtured the community under persecution and in exile. Mary's experience was blessed by a large number of these women, who made their prisons into schools and retreat houses and their homes into sanctuaries. Ursula Wright, Mary Ward's maternal grandmother, spent fourteen consecutive years in prison. Another of Mary's gallant kinswomen, Lady Grace Babthorpe, began married life at age fifteen with a two-year stint in jail; when she was arrested and asked how many Masses she had heard, "So many that I cannot count them" was her spirited response.[17]

In seeking this kind of life for women desiring to live consecrated lives, Mary Ward was in some ways seeking a freedom for single women that had long been the prerogative of wives: she wanted both the mobility of the heroic Jesuits who risked their lives to tend the Catholic flock in England—and the devotion of the heroic women who risked their lives to keep the Jesuits.

From her prison cell the night before she died, Margaret made a final bequest: she left her shoes to her eldest daughter, Anne, who was then twelve years old—and who, as a scholar in her mother's illegal school, had also been arrested and imprisoned following the raid. There is a strong motherly admonition implicit in the gesture. Follow in my footsteps, the wordless gift seems to say: carry on. Anne seems to have taken the hint: she was to be imprisoned again for "causes ecclesiastical" after her release at the time of her mother's death, and she later escaped an arranged marriage and made the hazardous journey to the Continent, where she became a nun in a Flemish convent. Like her mother before her, and like Mary Ward and her grandmother, Anne Clitherow chose the "old highway to heaven" and walked it faithfully.[18]

Mary Ward's shoes are similarly eloquent of steadfastness. Her worn leather shoes, in which she walked from Brussels to Rome, some fifteen hundred miles, are reverently displayed in the museum of the Institute house she founded in Altötting, Germany.

I am intrigued by these two pairs of shoes. I think they have much to teach us as we seek to know what it is to stand fast while moving forward. Our world, and our still-divided church, have changed in many ways in four hundred years, but both still need Christians with the wisdom and courage to persevere in what matters most.

These two women remind us that to stand fast is *not* to stand still. Steadfastness of purpose does not imply a heels-dug-in refusal to move into the future. Rather, to stand fast is to be deeply willing to continue on the way. We are called to be a pilgrim people, headed ever deeper into God on whatever highway we have chosen. Like Mary Ward and Margaret Clitherow, we may need to know when to speak truth to the powerful, when to live with failure, and even when to die in apparently ignominious defeat, planting what seeds we may, and entrusting to God and the future a harvest we will never see.

Pendle Hill

Chapter 9

Pendle Hill and George Fox

"Answering that of God in every one"

Fox's vision from the summit of Pendle Hill, less a private theophany than a prophetic call, linked heaven and earth.

—DAVID

I AM LOST. I had set out to climb Pendle Hill, and now I cannot even find it. Time is running out as well. I am due back at the Brontë Parsonage on Haworth Moor before dark to pick up Deborah and our daughters.

When I first heard of Pendle Hill in England's northwest county of Lancashire, I assumed it to be a rolling moortop, easily accessible by foot. I should have known better. I sought Pendle Hill because of its role in the life of George Fox (1624–91), and the Quaker had completed the ascent only "with much ado," as he recalled later in his *Journal,* "it was so steep."[1] An hour earlier I had at least caught sight of Pendle Hill in the distance. Snow-dusted and cloud-catching, the limestone ridge soared above small villages near its base, rising out of the lesser hills like the back of an enormous whale.

"Moved of the Lord to go up to the top of it" in the spring of 1652, a twenty-eight-year-old George Fox, son of a Puritan weaver father and a mother "of the stock of the martyrs," looked out into northwest England. "From the top of this hill the Lord let me see in what places He had a great people to be gathered,"[2] Fox wrote.

The vision from Pendle Hill would orient the rest of his life.

George Fox, solitary wanderer and disillusioned seeker, had paced restlessly about England, like a fast walker to a dead end. Dissatisfied with tepid answers to his fervent questions, stung by incongruous lives of preachers, he had found, he bemoaned, no one to "speak to my condition." Five years before Pendle Hill's commissioning vision, Fox's anguish with churchmen reached a climax:

> I cannot declare the misery I was in. . . . When all my hopes in them and in all men were gone, so that I had nothing outwardly to help me, nor could I tell what to do, then, oh, then, I heard a voice which said, "There is one, even Christ Jesus, that can speak to thy condition"; and when I heard it, my heart did leap for joy.[3]

Empty-handed and wearied, Fox encountered Christ in a series of revelations he called "openings." Like Julian of Norwich's "showings," these were not secondhand rumors of religion but experiences of the immediacy of divine love. Reaching the end of his rope, Fox found it attached to God. The ecclesial landscape through which Fox had wandered left little room for such firsthand experiences. Many Puritan churches held "that God had spoken to [humanity] through the scriptures and in the finished work of Christ," wrote the Quaker historian William Charles Braithwaite. "They believed that [God] would speak again in judgment at the second advent; meanwhile [we] ought not to look for further direct communication."[4]

It is arid terrain familiar to travelers from any age; thirsting for living water, they are handed empty canteens. Fox sloughed off doctrines like road dust. He turned his back on pastors, or to their consternation confronted them in midservice, indicting them for barren rhetoric. Seeing parishioners as resembling sleepwalkers, he roused and prodded them.

By the time he stood atop the 1,830-foot-high Pendle Hill, Fox had exchanged a private vision of a self to be saved for a great people to be gathered. As the Quaker writer Elfrida Vipont Foulds added, "It was as if he had suddenly received a new sense of direction in his wandering life."[5]

I do not seek my own vision (I tell myself) as I drive narrow back lanes toward Pendle. I go instead lured by Fox's story and his legacy of the Religious Society of Friends. I once assumed that *Friends* derived from the Quaker hallmarks of compassion and witness for peace. But the term originates in "Friends of the Truth"—truth being found, wrote Fox, "in God's voice speaking to the soul," in an encounter with one who said, "I no longer call you servants. . . . Instead, I have called you friends" (John 15:15, NIV).

Fox once wrote reassuringly, "I saw, also, that there was an ocean of darkness and death; but an infinite ocean of light and love, which flowed over the ocean of darkness. In that also I saw the infinite love of God, and I had great openings."[6]

Temptation being what it is, Fox might have begun with the experience of divine love only to disappear into the mists of quietism, like some ancient seeker of the Holy Grail inclined to "follow wandering fires! Lost in the quagmire," as one chronicler of the Grail legend observed, "And leaving human wrongs to right themselves, cares but to pass into the silent life."[7]

But, as Fox and other Quakers made clear, transcendent visions are not the goal. "Let us be quite clear that mystical exaltations are not essential to religious dedication," wrote the twentieth-century Quaker Thomas Kelly. "The crux of religious living lies in the *will*, not in transient and variable states. Utter dedication of will to God is open to *all* . . . Where the will to will God's will is present, there is a child of God."[8]

Fox's vision from Pendle Hill meant cells visited, hospitals cleansed, hungry fed, slaves freed, and wars spurned. I think of three Quakers in the southwestern United States welcoming a sixteen-year-old refugee from El Salvador's civil war, a massacre survivor who could not legally enter the United States. They pressed on him coffee and blankets. All half expected a constabulary knock at the door, handcuffs for the refugee. Years did not separate them from early Quakers. I watched their quiet attentiveness and obliviousness to the risk (born of their faith or history—or both?). In the refugee's eyes I detected a hint of repose: he knew he had landed among friends.

The Quaker movement may have been founded at Pendle Hill, but now Pendle Hill cannot be found by me. A curving road lined with hedges has led me down past farms into jangling Lancashire towns, more industrialized than they had appeared from a picturesque distance.

No signs alert drivers to Pendle Hill or the Quakers. When I asked directions from a farmer atop Haworth Moor, his only response had been, "Aye, Pendle Hill, it's the witches you'd be interested in then," referring to an alleged coven during the early seventeenth century when witch hysteria triggered the hanging of several women living near Pendle. My tourist map fails to distinguish between major and minor roads, and I have forgotten the name of the village nestled at the base of Pendle Hill that would offer easy footpaths leading to the summit. (It proves to be Barley, I learn much later, along with the name of the indispensable guidebook: *The Birthplace of Quakerism: A Handbook for the 1652 Country* by Elfrida Vipont Foulds.)

Thirty minutes of frenetic driving brings me only to a town somewhere northwest of Pendle Hill. I stop to ask directions. No one knows. Finally, a large, bright-eyed woman in her sixties nods when I mention the name. Shifting her shopping bag, she beams a broad smile and begins talking, rapidly giving me apparently precise instructions, but in a Yorkshire accent so thick as to be like Gaelic to me. I thank her, she smiles and moves on, and I point my car toward the nearest incline.

From my readings of Quakerism over the years (readings that skimped on road maps), one line in particular, familiar to every Quaker, resounds from George Fox. He wrote it from jail, his prison letter, in the tradition of the apostle Paul and Martin Luther King Jr., far outlasting his prison bars.

> Be patterns, be examples in all countries, places, islands, nations, wherever you come, that your carriage and life may preach among all sorts of people, and to them; then you will come to walk cheerfully over the world, answering that of God in every one.[9]

Whether we meet strangers, adversaries, or friends, we are to discern the "Light of Christ" within them. As Jessamyn West noted, "The truth Fox worked to bring to others was the possibility of a one-ness with Christ; and those who experienced this 'oneness' would demonstrate it by growing 'loving.'"[10] Such recognition, undermining our penchant for scorn, runs far deeper than mere mutual respect or humanist creed; perhaps Mother Teresa practiced it with the surest touch in our time.

"To answer that of God in every one" becomes a charge to the hearers, a benediction, and finally, one hopes, a way of life.

I follow a slender road leading upward, in the general direction of Pendle Hill. A sign promising a "View" reveals moments later only a mobile home park, commanding an airy perspective indeed but without giving a hint of Pendle's "long sloping flat top and chasmic sides," as described by Ronald Blythe in *Divine Landscapes,* the hill "treeless but evenly covered with cotton-grass, ling, mare's tail, butterwort, and with here and there a low bush of the aptly named cloudberry."[11]

As I drive fretfully on, suddenly my luck changes. Around a corner a country inn appears, and beside it a sign declaring "Footpath." I park the car and enter the inn, encountering a genial pubkeeper and his wife. Though dubious about my spying Pendle Hill from the moortop above, they assure me of a splendid view of Yorkshire's dales, and—pointing to a table by a wood fire—hot soup and a sandwich on my return.

I quickly set off up the hill on an ancient stone footpath ("part of an old Roman road," explained the innkeeper), delighted to be out of the car, walking briskly up the high, sloping pasture as air and sunshine poured over me.

Knowing time is short, calculating the hour of rendezvous with Deborah and our daughters, I occasionally break into a run up the hill. I pass drystone walls that enclose farmer's cottage and sheep-grazing lands, then open fields of heather with pools of clear water in the grass. Voices of other hill walkers echo over the distance, along with a low churning of a tractor. Climbing higher, beyond the walls, I reach what turns out to be a false summit, with a higher rise of moorland yet beyond that. Pendle Hill remains hidden.

I stop and turn around, breathing heavily. In the clear noon sky, I can see forty miles into Yorkshire and Lancashire. Green and yellow fields spread with sun stretch toward the Irish Sea. The disappointment I feel for missing Pendle Hill begins to be eclipsed by the realization that I am looking out on nearly the same view Fox did. The same dales, moor, and sun-stroked land. For the first time in hours, I stop moving and stand quietly as the wind rolls lightly over me.

Fox looked over this same scene from his loftier vantage and saw men and women waiting "to be gathered," to be yoked together by Christ into a people of prayer who would wait upon the Lord. "On Pendle he saw the size of his task as well as the only people who would be capable of helping him to complete it," recounts Ronald Blythe. "They were to be known as 'the valiant sixty' and nothing quite like their mission had been seen since Iona, Lindisfarne and other Celtic prayer-houses had sent their emissaries forth a thousand years earlier."[12]

The Quakers would know persecution. "They," wrote one of the best-known Friends, William Penn, "suffered great hardships for their love and good-will, being often stocked, stoned, beaten, whipt and imprisoned."[13]

Defiant, iconoclastic, tipping his hat to no one, disturbing decorum, dismissing oaths, and rejecting taxes, Fox offended and frightened. He himself was brought before the courts sixty times in thirty-six years, spending a total of six years in different prisons for heresy, plotting against authority, attending prohibited meetings, and refusing to take oaths or carry arms.

About fifteen thousand Friends faced legal sentences in the early decades; jail would imprison thousands, and death took the lives of hundreds in prison. "No cross, no crown," William Penn perceived, commemorating those who laid down lives instead of principles.

With Fox's emphasis on the inner life—rejecting pastors, doctrines, and sacraments while seeking out this mystical union—how did he hold himself accountable (and urge others to) so that it did not become untethered exaltation leading to spiritual anarchy?

For Fox, as for John Wesley nearly a century later, the answer lay in part within the community, a gathering of kindred souls, with trust that God would not let someone deep in prayer get too far away. The weekly Meeting would provide the framework.

From his vantage on Pendle, Fox might have glimpsed the folds of northwest England where the first Meetings would be held: villages such as Sawley, Settle, and Sedbergh, and far out of sight, Ulverston's Swarthmoor Hall, home of stalwart Margaret Fell, the mother of Quakerism (and eventual wife of George Fox), whose manor house would provide a harbor for early Quaker meetings.

"Quakerism is peculiar in being a group mysticism," wrote Howard Brinton in *Friends for 300 Years*.[14] The Meetings took place each week as Friends gathered to listen and wait upon the Lord in corporate stillness.

Accountability is one hallmark of a true visionary: after one recognizes the inner flame, one must create boundaries to check it from becoming wildfire. In the Quaker sense, this means one must test the voices in the tincture of silence.

⎯⎯

The Quaker movement began here. Or near here. It is probably just as well that I cannot climb Pendle Hill, cannot find the exact spot where God granted Fox a vision of a people to be gathered. Here, at a distance, I can only approach the outskirts of the story; disorientation keeps my presumption in check. Fox descended from Pendle not with sudden faith—faith he had known before—but with clearer purpose that seemed validated by God.

Fox's message would be echoed in the twentieth century by such spiritual descendants as Thomas Kelly (writing in *A Testament of Devotion* that "continuously renewed immediacy, not receding memory of the Divine Touch, lies at the base of religious living"[15]) and Elton

Trueblood. "We believe," Trueblood once noted with words simple in phrasing but staggering in significance, "that . . . Christ can be known now as truly as He was known by the disciples."[16] It is nothing less than the essential rediscovery of each age, indeed each day.

I wait in the noon sunlight. I hear distant voices of people—an older couple walking dogs on the high moorland. I listen for a more proximate, intimate voice. Even though I am unusually attentive, there is none. I receive no commissioning vision from this hill, and I begin the descent down through bracken and heather to my car and lunch.

Fox walked down from his Lancashire hill to speak God's word, to disturb the contented, to draw people from darkness to light. He would speak of the nearness of Christ to thousands in streets, hillsides, fields, prisons, cottages, and mansions.

As I walk down, a question comes to mind from this pursuit of Fox and Pendle: *Am I willing to speak to even one person?*

That is what I am left with in the sun of northern England. Not a commissioning but a question.

John Wesley's prayer room, London

Chapter 10

Aldersgate Street and John Wesley

"I felt my heart strangely warmed"

Dwarfed by office buildings and neglected by passersby, the memorial to Wesley's Aldersgate experience acts as a still, small voice in the London din.

—DAVID

I HAD ONLY a street name to go on: Aldersgate. I had no idea where it could be found in London. I knew the name solely by its reputation, linked irrevocably to John Wesley (1703–91) with the phrase "the Aldersgate experience." There on a spring evening in 1738, the founder of Methodism felt his heart "strangely warmed," an event that prompted a spiritual conversion that would transform not only eighteenth-century England but distant corners of the world.

Aldersgate Street occupied a place on the same map that charted conversions across history, from the apostle Paul's Damascus road to the corner of Fourth and Walnut Streets in Louisville, Kentucky, where a sense of overwhelming love for humanity broke in upon the Trappist monk Thomas Merton. In these and countless unnamed places, travelers have found themselves at the intersection of time and eternity.

I had hoped that the house on Aldersgate Street would still exist, perhaps lit by lantern or firelight. In one room there might be open on a polished table a copy of Luther's Preface to the Epistle to the Romans, turned to the page being read at the time of Wesley's conversion.

But none of this exists. The house itself, located in Nettleton

Court off Aldersgate Street, is gone, destroyed by World War II bombs that pulverized this portion of London. Serving as a fire watcher during the Blitz, the poet T. S. Eliot wrote of fine white ash suspended in air ("Dust inbreathed was a house"[1]), debris which one night might have included the Aldersgate dwellings.

This corner of London, now rebuilt, hosts massive office buildings and the Barbican complex with its shops, galleries, and theaters. Towers of concrete and steel block out the low winter sun, the icy city canyons magnifying the echo of traffic and jackhammers.

I have found no district of London more cluttered and inhospitable. To accommodate pedestrians, urban planners provided concrete walkways elevated above the streets. Near the entrance to the Museum of London, one of these open-air walkways leads past a memorial to John Wesley: a fifteen-foot-high bronze sculpture in the shape of a flame, imprinted with Wesley's words describing the Aldersgate experience. A small, water-stained sign at its base introduces the site: "This tablet is erected to the glory of God in Commemoration of the Evangelical Conversion of the Rev. John Wesley, M.A., on May 24, 1738."

I lean on the railing of the elevated walkway and look down into the street. A cold wind sends grit into my eye. Even before coming to London I held out no expectation of recreating Wesley's experience. Places are not vending machines that dispense transcendent insights. But I am unprepared for the thorough cacophony of this famed setting. It is like imagining the apostle Paul's conversion taking place on the New Jersey Turnpike.

Wesley little expected the experience to befall him at Aldersgate Street. At the time he was an Anglican priest filled with dissatisfaction, recently returned from having served as a missionary to America. His sojourn with the Society for the Propagation of the Gospel to the Indians had brought few converts. He confessed after his two and a half years in Georgia, "I went to America to convert the Indians; But Oh! who shall convert me?"[2] There lay on him, he wrote, a "strange indifference, dullness, and coldness, and unusually frequent relapses into sin."³ He seemed to be moving aridly through rituals while mouthing platitudes.

On the trip over to America, a violent storm—like the one that would shake the timbers of slave trader John Newton's disbelief—had split the mainsail and flooded the decks. Aboard ship, a group of Moravian Brethren, German Christians rooted in simple lifestyle and daily prayer, continued in their worship service. Impressed by their serenity amid the storm, Wesley later sought out the community. Arriving in Georgia, he went to the head of the small Moravian community for advice. There ensued one of the more renowned interchanges in Methodist history. The Moravian asked Wesley:

> "My brother, I must first ask you one or two questions. . . . Do you know Jesus Christ?" I paused, and said, "I know he is the Saviour of the world." "True," replied he, "but do you know he has saved you?" I answered, "I hope he has died to save me." He only added, "Do you know yourself?" I said, "I do." But I fear they were vain words.⁴

Wesley recounts the story in his *Journal;* most biographers mention it as well. With different people taking the two parts, the dialogue echoes down the centuries. I once found myself on Wesley's end, confronted by a Scottish evangelist, a wiry, silver-haired woman in her sixties. In virtually identical dialogue, she gently took the Moravian's role while I, backing away from her questioning, repeated Wesley's ringingly uncertain affirmation.

The January wind funnels down the walkway as I glance again at the sculpture. What tends to be forgotten in the Aldersgate event is Wesley's disclosure that he went "unwillingly" that spring evening. Resistance often seems a prelude to conversion: before the Damascus road, Paul resisted Christ by kicking "against the goads" (Acts 26:14); C. S. Lewis declared himself at Oxford to be the most reluctant convert in all England; George Herbert confessed by poem, "Love bade me welcome: yet my soul drew back, / Guilty of dust and sin."⁵ We stand on the brink of a deeper relationship with God, hesitating, wading in shallows when we are asked to swim.

The bronze memorial enlarges John Wesley's words from his *Journal* for passersby to read:

> In the evening I went very unwillingly to a society in Aldersgate Street, where one was reading Luther's Preface to the Epistle to the Romans. About a quarter before nine, while he was describing the change which God works in the heart through faith in Christ, I felt my heart strangely warmed. I felt I did trust in Christ, Christ alone for salvation, and an assurance was given me that he had taken away *my* sins, even *mine,* and saved *me* from the law of sin and death.[6]

Biographers record the event as nothing less than a watershed: "That great hour at the humble meeting in Aldersgate Street was certainly the turning point in Wesley's career. It marks the dividing line of his life."[7] "Henceforth he was never quite the same"[8]; Wesley now felt "the conquest of sin to be an assured fact, instead of being a "daily and almost hopeless struggle."[9] His brother Charles, living near Aldersgate, had just completed a hymn to celebrate his own conversion three days earlier and recorded in his journal: "Towards ten, my brother was brought in triumph by a troop of our friends, and declared, 'I believe.' We sang the hymn with great joy, and parted with prayer."[10]

It is possible, of course, to make too much of Aldersgate, to ignore promptings that preceded Aldersgate and faltering moments after it (when Wesley felt "much buffeted by temptations"). In the landscape of faith, conversion resembles not only a bridge but the road on either side of it, and Aldersgate winds long through Wesley's life.

As to the actual May 24 event, credit may as well trace back beyond the meeting to Luther's commentary on Romans, back further to the apostle Paul's letter to the Romans, and back still further to God. And that is the point. The incident itself can be overstated—but not the grace that undergirded it. The enduring meaning of Aldersgate is not so much our attentiveness as God's.

Despite the winter day and the windswept walkway, I am inclined to linger at Aldersgate Street, simply for its story. But I plan to meet my family in a few hours at Russell Square, and, before doing so, I have another destination in mind: Wesley's Chapel and House, located less than a mile away on City Road.

With map in hand, I round the corner of the sprawling Barbican complex, walking northeast, first along back streets, then through the green grass of Bunhill Fields, burial ground for such nonconformists as Daniel Defoe, William Blake, and John Bunyan. Wesley's mother, Susanna, is buried in the cemetery as well, but John lies outside its gates, across City Road behind the home where he lived for the last years of his life.

Dodging the traffic that hurtles down City Road, I enter the relative tranquility of the forecourt to Wesley's Chapel. Saved from a World War II bombing raid by a sudden shift in wind direction, the 1778 chapel anchors what one brochure calls "an acre of Christian heritage" that includes Wesley's statue, tomb, and narrow brick home. The chapel's crypt shelters the Museum of Methodism, its exhibits illuminating the rise of one of the largest Protestant denominations in the world.

Amid this cornucopia of Methodist lore and Wesleyan memorabilia, where to go first? I pause. For someone who has forgotten lunch, there is only one choice: a tea shop. Unfortunately the premises lack one, and instead I walk straight ahead, settling gratefully into a chapel pew for a moment of quiet.

If I were introducing a secular friend to John Wesley's legacy, a friend whom I presumed to be indisposed to hear Christ's name, I would pass over the lexicon of faith and fasten on Methodism's social witness. I would invoke the list of Wesley's accomplishments: the visits to the sick and those in prison; the schools, relief organizations, and loan funds initiated by Methodists. I would mention the famous exhortation attributed to John Wesley: "Do all the good you can, by all the means you can, in all the ways you can, in all the places you can, at all the times you can, to all the people you can, as long as ever you can."[11]

Not least, I would point out Wesley's free medical clinic and dispensary begun on City Road; his home for orphans; and his last letter, written about ten days before his death, to William Wilberforce, encouraging the fight against slavery.

It is tempting to fix attention solely on Wesley's curriculum vitae of humanitarianism. As with George Fox of the Quakers, the achievements at times overshadow the motivation.

And as all these good works were listed, Wesley (as he did in more than forty thousand sermons) would no doubt deflect attention away from himself, asking simply, "Why do you assume your friend is indisposed to hear the name of Christ?"

In the stillness of the well-lit chapel, near one of the jasper columns supporting the gallery, I look out on the pulpit that Wesley himself used. This church currently has over three hundred members in its multi-ethnic congregation. Here in this sanctuary, above a museum that charts the worldwide appeal of Methodism, it is easy to forget that Wesley had no intention of starting a new denomination. He remained an Anglican throughout his life, arguing that the societies he founded to provide encouragement and nurture were mere "auxiliaries" to the Church of England.[12]

Those who experience a firsthand conviction of God often seem to recognize the need for a framework that both supports and constrains them, that banks the fire lest, unchecked, it become wildfire. It might seem that the closer we draw to God the less we should need anyone else. But the "society," like the Quaker Meeting, Catholic monastery, or Anglican Church, reminds us of a paradox: The more we depend on God, the more we need community and accountability. Jesus is the shepherd, but we are notoriously vagrant sheep.

Next door to the chapel, an elderly guide, patient and well-versed, ushers me through the house where John Wesley lived when not traveling. In one room, pale January light washes over the peripatetic evangelist's belongings: a traveling robe, three-cornered hat, and traveling Communion set. Wesley often covered fifty miles a day by horse-back or carriage, his pace relentless as the springs of a clock. Offering words of deliverance, he preached what other priests had lost the ability to say or had never felt.

Though dedicated to John Wesley's memory, the house also displays his brother's bureau, study chair, and preaching bands. It was Charles's own deepening faith, culminating in a conversion on Whitsunday 1738, that not only quickened his brother's experience three days later at Aldersgate, but would bequeath one of the greatest legacies of hymnody in the world, his stanzas more familiar to posterity than any sermon preached by John.

Each hymn Charles wrote traces back to his personal experience of God's love and forgiveness. "I now found myself at peace with God," he wrote on May 21, 1738, "and rejoiced in hope of loving Christ."[13] Of his seven thousand hymns, two in particular bracket the year of Charles's own conversion: "Where Shall My Wondering Soul Begin?" written immediately after the event, and "O for a Thousand Tongues to Sing," drafted a year later on the first anniversary.

Launching the Evangelical Revival with an ark of words, the Wesleys spoke unabashedly out of the depth of their experience: "What we have felt and seen, with confidence we tell."[14]

My guide takes as much time for me alone as he would for a roomful of visitors. Thick walls muffle the sound of passing traffic on City Road, as oaken floors creak under our footsteps. Even though it is the off-season in London, I am surprised by how few people are here. This London destination remains off the beaten track, overshadowed by palaces, art museums, and theater marquees; Madame Tussaud's Waxworks hosts more visitors in a day than pass through here in a year.

Yet, of all Englishmen commemorated across the city, few surpass Wesley's influence in Britain and across the world. "The re-birth of the Christian religion in English history is directly traceable to John Wesley," noted one biographer.[15] Set against the backdrop of the fevered eighteenth century alone, the Methodist movement proved to be of "greater historic importance than all the splendid victories by land and sea won under Pitt," and steered Britain away from the shoals of revolution.[16]

Moreover, unlike the messages of many other orators, Wesley's theme has not faded. In his self-described quest "to beget, preserve and increase the life of God in the souls of [all]," Wesley preached of God's forgiveness and tenacious love. Of all the messages proclaimed by London's historic figures, none remains more contemporary.

The same question Wesley faced ("Do you know Jesus Christ has saved you?") stayed with me after being posed by the gentle, silver-haired Scottish evangelist. Discomforted by her question and uneasy with my tentative assent, I found myself turning over her query, examining its facets like a stone. I carried the question with me when I traveled to Iona not long thereafter, walking the island with a rare single-mindedness, repeating a prayer—"Help me to know that Jesus is my Savior"—that normally I would have shunned for its rigidity.

I half wanted any answer to be as swift as lightning and unmistakable as cloud letters arrayed in the sky, but the answer came quietly, unexpectedly, late in the day. I walked to the highest hill on Iona, its summit offering dazzling views over the Hebridean Sea, a setting as far from Aldersgate Street as could be imagined. It was as my words began to turn from petition to affirmation—as I found myself saying, "I believe that Jesus is my Savior"—that the knowledge sought indeed followed, like light entering an opened door. And I recalled the contours of a distant scriptural verse (that I traced back later to Paul's letter to the Ephesians): "For by grace you have been saved through faith, and this is not your own doing; it is the gift of God—not the result of works, so that no one may boast" (Eph. 2:8-9). Now as I write, I pull back from recounting the experience, lest it seem mechanistic or discontinuous with faith that undergirded me before. But I could sense then that beyond all that I did believe, something less shadowed could be known and indeed now was known.

With unwearied courtesy my guide takes time to show me the upstairs floors of Wesley's home, including the bedroom where Wesley is thought to have died in 1791. After ushering me into the adjoining "prayer room," he remarks as he withdraws, "I always like to let visitors have some time alone in here."

It presents a very small space, seven by eight feet, not much more than a closet, furnished simply with a chair, prayer stool, and table, its east-facing window now looking out on a London office building.

Wesley rose every morning at four o'clock and stepped into this quiet room to pray. "Here then I am, far from the busy ways of men," he wrote. "I sit down alone: only God is here. In His presence I open, I read His book."[17] Morning prayer aligned the day's trajectory, like a compass checked at dawn.

I find this unassuming room to be the most memorable niche in the cluster of buildings along City Road. More so than other corners of the house, this one seems to bring Wesley into focus, kneeling at morning prayers. In the stillness, one can almost hear an echo of Wesley's words on his deathbed: "The best of all is, God is with us."[18]

The guide returns after a few minutes and looks in on me, perhaps gauging whether I have added to the prayers offered in this room. It is late. Light is fading. Deborah and our daughters will be waiting for me near Russell Square. Thanking the guide, I make my way downstairs and close Wesley's door behind me as I step out into the London dusk.

Parish church, Olney

Chapter 11

Olney and John Newton

"Amazing grace, how sweet the sound"

With "Amazing Grace" and other Olney Hymns written from this market town, John Newton and William Cowper left a legacy of hymnody matched by few people and places in Christendom.

—DAVID

On a mid-December afternoon, I arrive in Olney, drawn to the English market town by a hymn. Following High Street past the Market Place, which is ablaze in Christmas decorations, I reach the parish church where the Reverend John Newton (1725–1807) once served as pastor.

The former captain of slave ships wrote hundreds of hymns from this landlocked town sixty miles north of London, his verses published along with those of his friend, the poet William Cowper, as the *Olney Hymns* in 1779. From this quiet corner of Britain emerged many of Christianity's most resounding hymns, among them "Faith's Review and Expectation," better known as "Amazing Grace":

> Amazing grace! How sweet the sound
> That saved a wretch like me!
> I once was lost, but now am found;
> Was blind, but now I see.

The hymn reflects precisely the life of the ex-slaver and Anglican curate who wrote it. John Newton had no mere vicarious acquaintance with gravity and grace. At Olney he penned his spiritual autobiography in five stanzas.

~

At the southeast wall of the churchyard, I find Newton's grave, its granite tomb incongruously imposing compared to the curate's self-effacing epitaph on its side:

> John Newton, Clerk,
> Once an infidel and libertine,
> A servant of slaves in Africa;
> Was, by the rich mercy of our Lord and Saviour, Jesus Christ,
> Preserved, restored, pardoned,
> And appointed to preach the Faith
> He had long laboured to destroy,
> Near sixteen years at Olney . . .

In prose and verse Newton proved a keen-eyed chronicler of youth's wasted hours, unflinchingly detailing his debauchery in a compelling literary mea culpa titled *An Authentic Narrative*. He had trafficked both in slaves and sins of the flesh, indulging in "the most abandoned scenes of profligacy." Like a doctor self-diagnosing a tumor, Newton pinpointed the source of his behavior as rebellion against God. On the eve of what would be his most eventful voyage between Africa and England, Newton wrote: "My whole life, when awake, was a course of most horrid impiety and profaneness. I know not that I have ever since met so daring a blasphemer: not content with common oaths and imprecations, I daily invented new ones."[1]

A stiff wind sweeps over Olney's churchyard, and winter light slants against the tomb's ironic letters: " . . . appointed to preach the Faith he had long laboured to destroy." Newton matched this confession in stone with an even more enduring one in song.

Newton wrote of amazing grace from this inland town, but he first experienced it on the high seas off Newfoundland. On board the *Greyhound* (a ship carrying not slaves but African beeswax, gold, and ivory to England) in March 1748, he chanced upon Thomas à Kempis's *The Imitation of Christ* in the captain's library, with its account of life's brevity and God's expectations. The following night a storm upended the North Atlantic, and as the twenty-two-year-old Newton struggled

at the wheel, he found an unaccustomed prayer for mercy on his lips—
"the first desire I had breathed for mercy for the space of many years."[2]

The storm shattered not only the ship but also Newton's old self.
Grappling with the vessel's wheel, pummeled with fear, the seaman could
have echoed John Donne's cry: "Batter my heart, three-person'd God."

The *Greyhound* survived, but it drifted for four weeks, reaching
Ireland's coast only as the "very last victuals was boiling in the pot."
Hours after the landing, the wind shifted so fiercely his ship would have
sunk had it still been at sea.

> Through many dangers, toils, and snares,
> I have already come;
> 'Tis grace hath brought me safe thus far,
> And grace will lead me home.

Some contemporary singers of "Amazing Grace" have assumed that
Newton's conversion immediately triggered a renunciation of slaving,
but he continued on for six years, only with time grasping its horror
and eventually helping to galvanize William Wilberforce and the
British antislavery movement.

Newton would not become an Anglican priest until sixteen years
after the *Greyhound's* voyage, and only slowly did this man of the sea
concede fully that he was not captain of his soul. Conversion for
Newton, as for most travelers, proved less an incident than a journey.
But having once caught a glimpse of grace from a tossing ship, Newton
kept it in view like the polar star.

John Newton may be one of Olney's most famous sons, but few of the
people I meet have him on their minds during the busy Christmas season. The local bookstore carries few titles about him. No monument
rises to him in Market Place's triangular green.

I attend the morning prayer service at the parish church of Saint
Peter and Saint Paul, its doors unlocked at the last minute by a fast-
peddling bicyclist, a middle-aged woman who introduces herself as a
deacon and morning reader. We take our places in the north aisle, the

only two worshipers this Saturday morning. Facing each other with prayer books in hand, we follow the liturgy, gradually overcoming our antiphonal awkwardness.

She takes time after the service to point out one of the few reminders of John Newton in the church—a stained-glass window depicting the curate in clerical garb flanked by a slave ship. In shadows at the back of the church, I find his old pulpit. When it came to pastoral visitation, Newton fed his congregation of largely poor lace makers with deep compassion, but he apparently lacked a talent for preaching. "His utterance," recalled one parishioner, "was far from clear and his attitudes ungraceful."[3]

If Newton's preaching lacked flair, his letters to correspondents on spiritual matters testify incisively to divine grace that lifts, restores, and unites. Called "the letter writer *par excellence* of the Evangelical Revival,"[4] Newton himself ventured, "It is the Lord's will that I should do most by my letters."[5]

Newton served for sixteen years here at Olney on the River Great Ouse, then for twenty-seven more years at London's Saint Mary Woolnoth, where he and his wife, Mary, moved for their second pastorate. When a friend urged rest near the end of his life, Newton replied, "I cannot stop. What, shall the old African blasphemer stop while he can speak?"[6]

If he rarely seemed at a loss for words, it was not so at first. After giving only six sermons at Olney, Newton "felt he had run through his whole stock," notes biographer Brian Edwards in *Through Many Dangers*.

> He wandered out of the churchyard and down to the Ouse; there he watched the river on its long journey to the sea. 'How long has this river run?' he thought. 'Many hundreds of years, and so it will continue. Is not the fund for my sermons equally inexhaustible—the Word of God?'[7]

One of the most haunting images from Norman Maclean's novel *A River Runs Through It* suggests that we often lack power to save those closest to us from self-destructive choices. But an even deeper truth echoes down through the centuries, spoken stubbornly by witnesses like Newton: not merely that we cannot save others, but that we cannot save even ourselves.

The rural countryside surrounding Olney unveils no stunning scenery, yet from this level landscape have risen two of the most monumental volumes in spiritual history: *The Pilgrim's Progress,* written in 1678 by John Bunyan in Bedford, a dozen miles east of Olney, and *Olney Hymns,* published in 1779 by Newton and his friend, the poet William Cowper.

"Once settled as Curate of Olney, Newton immediately made hymns a vital part of his ministry," notes D. Bruce Hindmarsh in *John Newton and the English Evangelical Tradition.*[8] Written on the far side of Newton's raw youth and in the throes of Cowper's recurrent melancholy, the 348 hymns were intended for the parish congregation's midweek prayer services and included Newton's "Glorious Things of Thee Are Spoken" and "How Sweet the Name of Jesus Sounds" and Cowper's "Sometimes a Light Surprises," "God Moves in a Mysterious Way," and "O! for a Closer Walk with God."

As Cowper himself reminded singers of *Olney Hymns,* any locale—whether obscure or breathtaking—can bring us closer to God; what saves us, after all, is not a place but a person:

Jesus, where'er thy people meet,
There they behold thy mercy seat;
Where'er they seek thee, thou art found,
And ev'ry place is hallow'd ground.[9]

In the center of the town, William Cowper's red-brick home now operates as the Cowper and Newton Museum. With serene gardens and Cowper's summer house for writing verse, much of the museum is given over to the famous poet's memorabilia and an exhibit of Olney's cottage industry of lace making. The museum devotes a single room to John Newton, displaying such items as his books, chairs, and clerical bands, and sells several hard-to-find books related to Olney's curate, including a collection of his letters.

"Through his conversion, narrative, his letters of spiritual direction, and his hymns, Newton's life became a potent symbol of the whole evangelical experience," observes D. Bruce Hindmarsh.[10]

According to a story I heard, a beloved Scottish doctor on his deathbed forbade any eulogy at his funeral. When asked why, he explained, "I've gone to too many funerals where the deceased was hailed as so wonderful that it sounded as if he had no need of a Savior." Like the Scottish doctor, John Newton made certain in the words he wrote that no one would make that mistake about him.

⟋⟍

The tune now associated with "Amazing Grace" came not from Newton's pen but from America, the folk melody (titled "New Britain") first linked with his text in 1835 in William Walker's *Southern Harmony.* It "is almost certainly Scottish in origin and was probably brought across the Atlantic by colonists in the eighteenth century," notes Ian Bradley, editor of *The Penguin Book of Hymns.*[11] The hymn thus spans the Atlantic, linking Old and New Worlds, as resonant on fiddle as on bagpipe.

"Yet 'Amazing Grace' is not nearly as popular here in England as in the U.S.," observes one Anglican priest, adding, "I suspect it has to do with our national heresy—Pelagianism—the sense that we can pull ourselves up by our bootstraps. Yanks across the Pond tend to be more realistic. Bootstraps are not enough."

At times "Amazing Grace" has acted like a bridge, allowing singers to cross over to an expression of repentance they otherwise would not care to utter. The author and retreat leader Evelyn Underhill once noted that her spiritual insights occasionally ran ahead of her actual experience: "I too arrive several years later at the experience of things I said."[12] With "Amazing Grace" we can find ourselves arriving several years later at the experience of the things we have sung.

When I was twenty-two years old and a disbeliever in Christianity, I worked for a year in Appalachia as both a teacher and a leader of a church youth group. One midwinter night I'd been asked to entertain a large gathering of coal miners and their families with my guitar and folk songs. To end, I'd chosen "Amazing Grace," a hymn I'd first come to know that year in the mountains of West Virginia. Midway through the second verse, I forgot the lyrics. The audience, raised as they had been on the hymn, filled in, singing even louder, until I recovered the words and we finished in unison. The incident turned out to be a metaphor for that year, a time of turning slowly to Christ: I stood before others to lead them in singing and ended by being taught the song.

In the years after I left Appalachia, I continued to sing "Amazing Grace," often with a classmate from law school. Our voices stretched out verses like taffy, as my friend's Baptist upbringing elongated the comfort of salvation. After our marriages, our wives joined in, and the four of us would end evenings together singing it *a cappella*—a Baptist, Presbyterian, Catholic, and Episcopalian—all brought together around the fire of "Amazing Grace."

My daughters were exposed early to the hymn (asking to hear "Mary Grace" as though it were a nursery tune about yet another Mary). I would wince, however, when my young—and to a father, forever innocent—daughters would sing "that saved a wretch like me," the tone discordant in such tender lives.

Old age does not prevent an eighty-year-old friend from loathing the hymn for language she considers self-abasing. Some hymnals substitute *soul* for *wretch,* while other writers have tried to revise the verse, one venturing into dubious theology and syntax: "Amazing grace, how sweet the sound, that shone a jewel like me."

Yet the words as first drafted by Newton still ring true; we are indeed a people who have slipped far from God. But the point is God's forgiveness, not our fallenness. We rise to sing "Amazing Grace," not "Amazing Sin."

In Olney, John Newton is no more. Only a tomb and a few dusty mementos survive. Olney offers a sharp rebuke to the presumption of earthly immortality: he is not here, he has risen.

I don't doubt that Newton would approve of time having eclipsed his name. It is more than enough to have bequeathed such words as "Amazing grace, how sweet the sound" that rise without protest to our voices, so that in singing we remember less the composer than the Author of grace itself.

A few weeks before he died on December 21, 1807, John Newton remarked to a visitor, "My memory is nearly gone; but I remember two things: that I am a great sinner, and that Christ is a great Saviour."[13]

The ship on the high seas has stopped tossing. The storm is over. And we find ourselves anchored in the fathomless mercy of God.

Woodland, St. Beuno's

Chapter 12

St. Beuno's and
Gerard Manley Hopkins

"Steady as a water in a well"

Even if you don't have time for a retreat at St. Beuno's, try to walk awhile up the hill behind the house. And by all means go to nearby Holywell to experience firsthand the trembling icy waters of Saint Winefred's spring.

—DEBORAH

To WALK THE HILLS in the north of Wales in the early spring is inevitably—at least for this English major—to think of Gerard Manley Hopkins (1844–89). Here at St. Beuno's College, Hopkins studied theology as a young Jesuit from 1874 to 1877. Here, in response to this landscape that he found full of God's grace, he composed his most lyrical poems.

"Nothing is as beautiful as Spring," I quote exuberantly to myself as I climb through the woods to the high green pastures. Listening, amazed, I wholeheartedly agree that a warbling thrush

> Through the echoing timber does so rinse and wring
> The ear, it strikes like lightnings to hear him sing.[1]

Hopkins exulted in the wild beauty of this place, not just the glories of the earth but of the sky as well:

> . . . up above, what wind-walks! What lovely behaviour of silk-sack clouds![2]

131

I wonder if it was from one of these wind-swept pastures that he caught sight one morning of a falcon riding the wind with such powerful grace that he exclaimed in wistful admiration of "the achieve of, the mastery of the thing!"[3]

From the slopes of Maenefa, the hill that rises behind St. Beuno's, I can see the long, honey-colored bulk of the college riding like a ship at anchor below me. "The house stands on a steep hillside," Hopkins reported in a letter to his father soon after his arrival; "it commands the long-drawn valley of the Clwyd to the sea, a vast prospect."[4]

The college was built in 1849 ("of limestone, decent outside, skimping within, Gothic, like Lancing College done worse"[5]) at the height of Victorian delight in pseudomedieval architecture, which indulged in fantasies of mystery and intrigue. The enormous building is constructed, confusingly enough, around two courtyards, with a labyrinth of wide corridors that narrow and divide and turn corners, running up and down unexpected half flights of stairs as unpredictably as mountain streams.

Once, after several days on retreat at St. Beuno's, I absentmindedly took an unaccustomed stairway up from the library in the basement and found myself in a wholly unfamiliar part of the house, with no apparent access to the known. I felt almost as startled as Alice suddenly thrust through the looking glass, and had to creep down several flights of stairs to undo my navigational error. It comforts me to know that these architectural fancies also bewildered Hopkins: "The staircases, galleries, and bopeeps are inexpressible: it takes a fortnight to learn them."[6]

～

When Hopkins arrived at St. Beuno's in the summer of 1874, he was thirty years old, having joined the Society of Jesus six years before. Physically slight and frail, intellectually and spiritually intense and complicated, he struggled all his life with ill health and depression, although he also had great courage and a startling capacity for joy. A devout convert to Catholicism, Hopkins was passionate about beauty and language, which naturally led him as an undergraduate to the writing of poetry.

Hopkins resolved, before he entered the Jesuit novitiate, to stop writing poems; in fact he burned the verses he had already written.[7] He knew that his extreme sensitivity to beauty could distract him from his priestly work, so he resolved to "give up all beauty until I had [God's] leave for it."[8] For six years he wrote no poetry at all, beyond a few incidental pieces composed—frequently in Latin—at the request of his superiors to mark some special occasion within the community.

Then, in December 1875, when Hopkins had been at St. Beuno's for only a few months, an unlikely event—a shipwreck on the other side of Britain—broke the great silence. A German ship bound for America foundered on a sandbank in the mouth of the Thames. Many passengers died, including five Franciscan nuns exiled by anti-Catholic legislation. Hopkins, reading of the disaster in the London *Times,* was deeply affected by the incident; he spoke of it to the rector, who remarked that he wished someone would write a poem about it. This hint was apparently all the permission Hopkins needed. He began at once to write the most ambitious poem he ever attempted, *The Wreck of the Deutschland.*[9]

The large community room where the fateful conversation between Hopkins and the rector took place that winter night, well over a century ago, looks today much as it must have done then: tall windows looking over the valley, a huge cavern of a fireplace, now tidily bricked into a more manageable size. I enter the house from the garden (carefully scraping the mud of the hills from my boots) and stand a few moments before the now-cold grate to salute that distant moment, and then head upstairs to the refectory for lunch.

The refectory, like all the rooms I have seen in the college (as I keep thinking of it, although it is now known as St. Beuno's Ignatian Spirituality Centre[10]), is large and handsome, with high mullioned windows. The table to which I am assigned a place for meals, where the "high table" for the rector and staff once stood, stands directly beneath the formidable carved wooden pulpit, set in the wall about six feet from the floor. As part of their training, theology students in Hopkins's day—indeed well into the twentieth century—took turns preaching to the gathered community at supper. I eat my own meal in solitude (to the accompaniment of taped classical music), wincing to remember what a disaster Hopkins felt one of his sermons from that pulpit to have been.

Hopkins had taken as his text the Gospel story of the loaves and fishes, which he elaborated in a painstakingly didactic way. For instance, in "composing the place" in good Ignatian fashion, he earnestly proposed that the Sea of Galilee was "shaped something like a . . . man's left ear; the Jordan enters at the top . . . and runs out at the end of the lobe. . ."[11] Hopkins's hearers apparently found this earnest explication absolutely hilarious. Hopkins himself noted, with more bewilderment than irritation,

> People laughed at it prodigiously. I saw some of them roll on their chairs with laughter. This made me lose the thread, so that I . . . mixed things up. . . . [which] made them roll more than ever.[12]

If unorthodox as a preacher, as a poet Hopkins was simply unknown. Although he is commemorated today in the Poets' Corner of Westminster Abbey, the obituary that appeared in the *Journal of British Jesuits* after his death in Dublin in 1889 mentions his poetry not at all. The tone of the obituary is careful; one senses charity at odds with candor. Words like *quaint, peculiar,* and *eccentric* vie with the likes of *gentle* and *lovable.* Hopkins's life seems to have been a lonely one. As he put it himself toward the end of his life,

> To seem the stranger lies my lot, my life
> Among strangers.[13]

It is common among Hopkins's biographers to call his years at St. Beuno's the happiest of his life, and indeed, from the record of his letters, journals, and poems, that seems to be true. But it seems to have been the hills and pastures and streams of Wales—always to him "a mother of Muses"—that appealed to him so strongly rather than his fellow students or the course of study.[14] "Wild Wales breathes poetry," he claimed.[15] It is frequently assumed that "the house where all were good to me" (fondly remembered in "In the Valley of the Elwy") is St. Beuno's itself. However, Hopkins clearly refutes this assumption in a letter to his Oxford friend, Robert Bridges, elucidating the poem. While Hopkins did have one or two close friends among his classmates at St. Beuno's, it would be odd for him to have characterized the place as one "where all were good to me."[16]

Furthermore, he doubtless would have been astounded by the suggestion that they should have been. Hopkins had not converted to Catholicism nor joined the Society of Jesus in order to find people who would be "good to him," but in order to "praise, reverence, and serve God," the purpose for which human beings were created, according to Ignatius Loyola, founder of the Jesuits.[17]

Hopkins was a Jesuit to the marrow of his bones. He never regretted his vocation for a moment, although he suffered anxiety over his apparent failures, his recurrent sickness and low spirits, his felt inability to sustain "the achieve . . . the mastery" he so admired in others. "I do not waver in my allegiance, I never have since my conversion to the Church," he wrote in his journal during the last retreat of his short life. "The question is how I advance the side I serve on."[18]

Hopkins's celebrated love of nature was built firmly upon his deeply Ignatian conviction that the whole world is full of God. As he put it himself:

All things . . . are charged with love, are charged with God,
and if we know how to touch them give off sparks and take fire,
yield drops and flow, ring and tell of him.[19]

Hopkins had been afraid, before he entered the Jesuits, that to attempt to be both a priest and a poet would be to live somehow in conflict with himself and with God's will for him. But both desires were aspects of his one vocation, springing from a deep interior source. His conviction that everything in creation was intended to utter forth the Creator's name and praise was central both to his religious faith and his poetic theory; he believed that everything was created to "give beauty back" to its Creator.[20] This inherent purpose was inextricably, joyfully, associated with each creature's identity:

> As kingfishers catch fire, dragonflies draw flame;
> As tumbled over rim in roundy wells
> Stones ring . . .
> . . . .
> Each mortal thing does one thing and the same:
> Deals out that being indoors each one dwells;
> Selves – goes itself; *myself* it speaks and spells,
> Crying *What I do is me: for that I came.*[21]

Perhaps nowhere is this perception of the intimate, graced bond between Creator and creation, between meaning and identity, more apparent than in Hopkins's extravagant love of water in all its native forms—streams, pools, raindrops, oceans—and his special devotion to the myriad holy wells and pools of North Wales. Hopkins frequently made these "roundy wells" the object of a walk on the weekly holidays when the theology students were "free to go out for the day with sandwiches, but without money."[22]

There are nearly one hundred wells dedicated to the Virgin Mary in Wales, and many others associated with Saint Winefred, the niece of Saint Beuno, the Welsh saint for whom the college was named. St. Winefred's Well at Holywell, a few miles from St. Beuno's, has been venerated as a healing spring since at least the eleventh century. It became a regular place of pilgrimage for Hopkins, and "came to mean more to [him] than anything else in Wales."[23]

Hopkins wrote to Bridges:

> Who was St. Beuno? Is he dead? Yes, he did that much 1200 years ago, if I mistake not. He was St. Winefred's uncle and raised her to life when she died in defense of her chastity and at the same time called out her famous spring, which fills me with devotion every time I see it . . . the flow of [the bright water] is so lavish and beautiful.[24]

Hopkins's journal for 1874 records his first momentous visit to the well. He and a fellow student

walked over to Holywell and bathed at the well and returned very joyously. The sight of the water in the well as clear as glass, greenish like beryl or aquamarine, trembling at the surface with the force of the springs . . . quite drew and held my eyes to it. . . . The strong unfailing flow of the water and the chain of cures from year to year all these centuries took hold of my mind with wonder at the bounty of God in one of His saints, the sensible thing so naturally and gracefully uttering the spiritual reason of its being (which is all in true keeping with the story of St. Winefred's death and recovery) . . . even now the stress and buoyancy and abundance of the water is before my eyes.[25]

Hopkins's visits to Saint Winefred's shrine at Holywell were all on foot—some twelve rough miles of hill walking each way—but I make my less stalwart way by village taxi. Hundreds of Catholic pilgrims from all over the world still visit every year; it is in fact one of the few places of unbroken pilgrimage across the centuries remaining in Europe. Thus I am surprised, this bright February afternoon, to have the place to myself.

I have it, in fact, all too thoroughly to myself: the high iron gates are padlocked shut, and a note stuck to them informs me that the shrine is closed; the curator has "Gone to a funeral—back at 2 P.M." I wait fifteen minutes past the appointed hour of return and then, when still no curator appears and still the taxi waits, I stealthily climb the fence and drop to the grassy lawn on the other side.

Perhaps because of my purloined entry, or the solitude, or the silence, or the breezy, cloud-chased changeable light, I am much struck by the unearthly atmosphere of the place.

The vaulted interior of the tiny chapel, built over the well itself in the early 1500s, is cool and dim on this sun-shot day, the flames of votive candles guttering in the wind. Slender stone columns support the carved roof. The effect is both sheltered and airy—alive.

The water pours out of the stony depths of the spring to fill the star-shaped stone well and then, overflowing, the long rectangular pool set like a jewel in the velvet lawn. It is indeed clear as glass, pale green, "trembling at the surface with the force of the springs." I kneel to dip a hand in the water, and snatch it back quickly: it is breathtakingly cold and moves with the current like a living thing against my fingers. Standing in that quiet empty place by myself, with the tremulous crystal spring murmuring its ancient song to itself, I almost feel time stop and disappear.

With all my heart and all my senses, I understand the charm of this whole place to Hopkins—the delicate stone columns, the long pool, the candles—but I feel sure it was the spring itself, representing the responsiveness of nature to God—"so . . . gracefully uttering the spiritual reason of its being"—that he loved most. The water in that well—"stressed and buoyant and abundant"—was doing spontaneously what it was created to do, "give beauty back," which Hopkins saw as the universal vocation of all creatures, and which he found so poignantly difficult. The spring became a powerful sign, both symbol and example, of the mysterious grace of God alive and active in the world God loves.

Returning to St. Beuno's from Holywell, I find I am reluctant to leave behind the spell of airy mystery cast by the well, and console myself for its loss by flinging wide the window of my room. I lift my face to the strong river of evening air that pours through. The February twilight is deeply blue and smells of rain; the tonic air fresh from Snowdon is animated, ruffling the papers spread across my desk. It is also freezing. I wrap myself in the bedspread and curl up in the large armchair under the lamp, settling down with my battered volume of Hopkins's poems.

Browsing through the book, I come upon a favorite stanza from *The Wreck of the Deutschland* and unexpectedly find myself back at St. Winefred's Well:

> I steady as a water in a well, to a poise, to a pane,
> But roped with, always, all the way down from the tall
> Fells or flanks of the voel, a vein
> Of the gospel proffer, a pressure, a principle, Christ's gift.[26]

These four lines express in remarkably succinct form not only classic Christian reliance in faith on the love of God in Christ, but also the characteristically Ignatian insistence on God as powerfully active in the world, and in fact as "pressing" us to respond to that love, which we can never merit but only receive as "Christ's gift."

Hopkins takes the image of a spring-fed well, filled by sources beneath the surface, and joins it with that of a mountain pool (*voel* is Welsh for mountain), fed by sources high above it. In both cases, the apparently still water on the surface is connected—"roped with, always"—the living source that sustains and replenishes it. Hopkins realizes himself to be similarly "roped with"—fed, sustained, supported by—the grace of God.

He "steadies" himself on the surface "as a water in a well, to a poise," a dynamic stillness, apparently smooth as a "pane" of glass. At the same time however, he is forever linked with the "gospel proffer"—in other words, grace—which he experiences not only as support but as "a pressure"—in striking parallel echo of his journal entry describing the "stress, buoyance, and abundance" of the water in St. Winefred's Well.

There is sometimes a wistful note in Hopkins's poetry that reveals he considered himself to have failed to do what God had asked of him, while admiring "the achieve . . . the mastery" of others: he was often more conscious of the "stress" rather than the "buoyancy" or "abundance" of his vocation.

St. Winefred's Well was not only an exquisite thing, existing in perfect integrity with its purpose in having been created ("so naturally and gracefully uttering the reason for its being"); it was also a healing spring, its waters credited with miraculous powers of restoration. The spring existed, in the language of the Book of Common Prayer, not only for the glory of God, but for the welfare of God's creatures, not only to praise and reverence but also to "serve" God.[27] Hopkins, in identifying with the blessed water in the well (and incidentally in writing about it) recognizes himself, for once, to be doing the same thing, similarly "uttering the reason for his being."

And so he did to the end of his days. He "advanced the side he served on" not only as a priest among the the urban poor of Dublin and Liverpool, living daily the difficult response of "courage and generosity" that Ignatius urges, but also as a passionately faith-filled poet whose work has "steadied," nourished, and illumined the lives of thousands.[28]

In the image of the well, where Hopkins identifies himself with the water—tremulous, fluid, dynamic, part of the great mystery of creation responsive to the Creator—he perhaps most clearly unified within himself both priest and poet. Here for a moment one can almost hear the confluence of the two vocations, like two great rivers triumphantly pouring into one.

The main chapel at St. Beuno's has been extensively renovated since Hopkins's day, but strong traces of its Victorian splendor remain: The same carved angel corbels that looked down from the vaulted heights on Hopkins's ordination here in 1877 still fold their wings along the roof beams. The same nineteenth-century stained-glass windows, now luminous in morning light, portray the story of Saint Beuno and Saint Winefred, uncle and niece, honoring the mysterious spring of healing water flowing from the earth. The flame of the sanctuary lamp still burns steadily beside the altar. Above all, the atmosphere of dynamic stillness, of prayerful listening, evokes Hopkins's life and spirit— "stressed, buoyant, and abundant."

As I settle on my knees in the charged silence, I close my eyes behind my hands and recall the gem-clear water of St. Winefred's Well. I remember seeing pools in the high Welsh meadows, constantly replenished by the narrow silver waterfalls flashing down from unseen sources in the mountains. As the stillness and the blessing deepen around me, I recall other times and places when, like Hopkins, indeed like "water in a well," I also have been powerfully and mysteriously acted upon by grace. I realize gratefully that, here, for a moment, in this place where Hopkins vowed himself to "praise, reverence, and serve God," I too can be "steady as a water in a well"—because I am (thanks be to God) "roped with, always, all the way down. . . . Christ's gift."

Pleshey Retreat House garden

Chapter 13

Pleshey and Evelyn Underhill

"A house soaked in love and prayer"

In the house's lovely garden, you can see the ruins of the tiny Saint Francis oratory that stood there in Evelyn Underhill's time. The crumbling stone walls are overgrown with roses now: it remains a peaceful place for prayer.

—DEBORAH

SILENCE AND PEACEFULNESS as tangible as bread welcome me as I cross the threshold of the Retreat House at Pleshey, beloved of Evelyn Underhill more than half a century ago. The fragrance of freshly baked bread, just out of the oven in the kitchen off the entryway, does in fact warm and scent the autumn afternoon. Pots of rose geraniums grow on the broad sunny windowsill of the landing; the domestic incense of just-baked bread and the peppery freshness of rose geranium leaves follow me as I climb to my room (named Charity) at the top of the stairs.

Aside from the warden and other staff, I am alone in the house. By a graced coincidence, my three-day visit—part pilgrimage, part retreat—falls on a rare blank in the diocesan calendar. I exult in the quiet solitude and in the chance to prowl around by myself. Upstairs, opening off wide corridors, some twenty single bedrooms on two floors tidily await their next occupants, their casement windows looking placidly out on the fields and woods of the Essex countryside. On the ground floor, in addition to the warm, fragrant kitchen, are a large refectory and a couple of pleasantly furnished meeting rooms, as well as a handsome Edwardian library with Evelyn's books, all first editions, on the shelves, and her Italian crucifix in a window.

A framed piece of embroidery, which Evelyn once kept on her desk, is propped on the library mantel: it has the single word *ETERNITY* worked in blue wool on white linen. A powerful reminder of the context of our lives, it offers silent counterpoise to the peaceful ticking of the old-fashioned clock nearby.

As I wander from peaceful room to room, I remember C. S. Lewis's description of his childhood home: a house, like Pleshey, full of "long corridors, empty sunlit rooms, upstairs indoor silences."[1]

I am also deeply, delightfully aware of the memory of Evelyn Underhill, pervasive as the scent of rose geraniums. She dearly loved this house, where she conducted retreats from the mid-1920s to the mid-1930s. It is because of her that I am here.

I first encountered Evelyn Underhill's name on the spine of a book in a church library many years ago when I was browsing at random among texts on mystical theology—a subject that interested me at that time in a remote and faintly wistful way, just as someone on crutches might choose to read about ascents of Everest. I pulled down Evelyn Underhill's book *The Mystics of the Church,*[2] knowing nothing about her at all, not even gender (having once been startled to discover that Evelyn Waugh was a man).

Standing in that quiet library, flipping through *The Mystics,* was one of those moments that, although one has no idea of it at the time, begin to change one forever. The book is a collection of short biographies of the giants of Christian prayer, from the apostle Paul to Teresa of Avila, from Meister Eckhart to Mechthild of Magdeburg. The scholarship is impeccable, the bibliography formidable, but the warmth of tone struck me, especially the implicit—and transforming—assumption that these great souls were our companions on the pilgrim way. Evelyn Underhill made holiness and unitive prayer seem not an Everest impossibility but a marvelous personal invitation, almost a birthright. Flipping through the pages of that book was like leafing through a family album of beloved ancestors—encountering real people whom one might not have met in Time but to whom, nonetheless, one was really related in Eternity. I read the book from cover to cover and went on greedily to read everything by Evelyn Underhill that I could find.

The vein of gold running through all her books has always been, for me, the same pure metal I found in *The Mystics of the Church:* her "delighted confidence"[3] that a life of prayer is a great adventure, an invitation into a transformed and transforming relationship with the Author of the universe, a chance to engage with all the company of heaven in the redemption of all things, a chance for our souls to "breathe the atmosphere of Eternity," which is their "native air."[4]

Evelyn Underhill makes contemplative prayer seem immensely attractive and exciting: "We stand on the verge of a great world of possibility," she declared.[5] It was to keep this reality before her that she kept the needlework reminder *ETERNITY* on her desk, as an outward sign of that inward grace.

Evelyn Underhill was the first person to help me believe in the glorious possibility that while yet confined to the narrow swift-flowing river of chronological time, we are by grace invited to join God in *kairos,* the unbounded infinite sea of eternity—not merely for our own delight, but for the great privilege of joining God in loving the world into the Kingdom.

⌐‿

Largely self-taught in the field of mystical theology, Evelyn wrote or edited thirty-nine distinguished books on the nature and practice of mysticism, produced over 350 book reviews and articles, and was in great demand as a lecturer for church and academic societies. She was a fellow of King's College, London, and received an honorary Doctor of Divinity degree from the University of Aberdeen. She was, as Charles Williams has noted, "one of the most widely read writers on prayer and the spiritual life in the first fifty years of the twentieth century."[6] She was most loved and is best remembered, however, as a spiritual guide and retreat director. Nearly a dozen of her published works—some of the most influential in my own life—are, in fact, addresses from retreats she conducted at Pleshey.

Her own first retreat at Pleshey produced an effect so profound and pivotal that it amounted to a conversion experience.[7] In the early 1920s she was acquiring a reputation as an "expert" in the field of mystical theology—she was the first woman invited to give a series of lectures on religion at Oxford, for instance. However, ironically and sadly, her own spiritual life was in crisis at that time. Perhaps as knowledgeable as anyone in Europe about the treasures of Christian mystical theology, she found herself increasingly isolated, both intellectually and spiritually. The life of prayer, so important to her at so many levels, seemed more and more, at this time, a life she shared with no one else. Neither her husband (an agnostic solicitor) nor her parents (a prosperous Victorian barrister and his wife) had any interest in religion.

Evelyn's ostensibly sheltered and even successful life during the war years of 1914–1918 was interiorly shattering: "During the war I went to pieces," she reported cryptically to her spiritual director, Baron von Hügel. She, like many sensitive Christians, was appalled by the brutality of war. Also, despite her vast learning and (more or less secret) life of prayer, she had no real spiritual home, no anchor, no larger context or discipline within which she might have found strength or meaning.

The end of the war found her in a state of exhaustion, confusion, and deprivation. She had long felt drawn to the Catholic Church but excluded by obedience to family opposition (and, eventually, by personal intellectual misgivings about the rigid orthodoxy that characterized Catholicism at the time). At the same time, however, she could not fully claim her place in the Anglican communion of her birth; her friend Lucy Menzies mused ruefully that Evelyn as a young woman "experienced the best of the church of Rome but never the best of the Church of England."[8] Consequently Evelyn—a great lover of God and scholar in the giants of the faith—was increasingly self-exiled from either church and cut off from sacramental life and the possibility of community that might have sustained her.

She was, in fact, as she herself would later put it, suffering the strain and fatigue of living her spiritual life with all the windows shut: "How horribly stuffy and exhausted . . . our religious atmosphere gets sometimes: how utterly we forget that we live and move and have our being in a God Who fills the whole universe."[9]

In 1921 "this brilliant unyoked creature"[10] had placed herself under the direction of the formidable von Hügel, to whom she confessed herself to be "frantic and feverish . . . I had times of the blackest depression, when it seemed the strain could not be borne, or the utter loneliness. Religion seemed suddenly to have become savage and unrelenting."

Her letter to von Hügel continues: "Then at Ascension tide I went into retreat at Pleshey."[11] She loved the place at once.

⸻

So do I.

I feel as if I am returning to a beloved place, rather than arriving for the first time. I stand at the window of Charity for a while, looking out over the garden and the chapel below, savoring the serenity. Even now, in November, a mild and mellow peacefulness pervades the moated garden, along with the scent of fallen apples, raked into tidy piles around the trunks of the mother trees.

My room at the head of the stairs has a massive oak door with a medieval creak and a huge brass knob at shoulder height. Plush curtains on brass rings hang by the deep leaded windows; the bed is narrow but comfortable; the lighting is good. The house was built in 1906, but the effect is calmly, solidly Gothic.

"The whole house seems soaked in love and prayer," Evelyn wrote to von Hügel after her first retreat. "To my surprise a régime of daily communion and four services a day with silence between was the most easy unstrained and natural life I had ever lived." Significantly, the experience did not so much provide a haven of solitude, a withdrawal from the claims of others, as it corrected an inner isolation and reconnected her with the larger church. She wrote to von Hügel that the retreat "cured" her solitude. "I lost there my last bit of separateness and . . . came away quite tranquil. . . . My old religious life now looks . . . thin and solitary."[12]

Evelyn's first retreat at Pleshey was to root and ground her in a number of significant ways. It nourished and steadied her private prayer; it put her in sustaining touch with the whole church through participation in the divine office. It also gave her a sense of belonging in the Anglican Church for the first time and put an end to her agonized ecclesiastical restlessness, her sense of not being at home in either the Roman or the Anglican Church. In the same post-Pleshey letter to von Hügel she writes, "I feel now quite satisfied as an Anglican; having discovered a corner I can fit into, and people with whom I can sympathise and work."

By the summer of 1922, Evelyn was clear about both her ecclesiastical affiliation and religious vocation, and Pleshey became an emblem of both. At an even deeper level, the retreat at Pleshey had reconnected her with God and with herself by opening the windows of her mind and heart to the pure air of Eternity.

In 1924 she wrote to a friend, "I have just been asked to conduct a three day retreat at my dear Pleshey in Lent. . . . It seems a great responsibility, but I think I have to do it. Of course the Chaplain will say Mass each day but I shall take all the addresses, meditations and interviews. So you must pray for this too."[13]

Henceforth, Evelyn steadfastly championed the retreat movement within the Church of England, and herself led about eight retreats a year, usually three of them at Pleshey. T. S. Eliot felt that the awareness within Evelyn of "the grievous need of the contemplative element in the modern world" was the sustaining inspiration of all her work.[14]

Evelyn knew—she had learned the hard way—that our spiritual lives, no matter how committed to God and the work of the Kingdom, can become cramped and dry, worn out to the point of breakdown, if we try for too long to go without breathing our "native air of Eternity." That is why, I think, she was always such a firm advocate of annual retreats for those engaged in ministry.

In 1932 Evelyn addressed the annual meeting of the Association for Promoting Retreats. She began by saying, "A first retreatant lately told me that when she confessed to her husband what she intended to do, he took his pipe from his mouth and said earnestly: 'Go, my dear. Go, by all means! You're just about due for a spot of re-birth.' That man, it seems to me, had a very clear idea of one function of a retreat: its power of causing the re-birth of our spiritual sense, quickening that which has grown dull and dead in us, calling it out into light and air, giving it another chance."[15]

In the clear light and air of this November afternoon, I close the door of Charity and head for the chapel. I wonder, on the way, what Evelyn would have thought of my having been (no doubt randomly) assigned to that particular room—would she have put me in Patience or Fortitude instead? I know she herself named the rooms and always gave careful thought to the room assignments when she was preparing for a retreat. She usually arrived at Pleshey at least a day in advance to post the meditation texts, assign rooms, arrange flowers for the library and hall, and prepare the chapel.

Lucy Menzies, a close friend of Evelyn's and for many years warden at Pleshey, remembered that when Evelyn came to lead a retreat,

> everything down to the smallest detail was thought of and arranged beforehand, so that the whole mind and heart and soul of all present might be fixed wholly upon God. E.U. would be found in the porch of the chapel soon after she arrived, putting up all particulars—suggestions for Bible readings, Points for Meditation, times for interviews, the Hymn Sheet, etc. (She was very particular about hymns, which were carefully chosen for each Address—and woe betide the organist if the hymns dragged!)[16]

Perhaps that is why I feel so close to Evelyn now: the house must have felt like this—quiet, expectant, empty—when she arrived to prepare for a retreat. I find myself checking the bulletin board for her neatly posted lists, and being irrationally disappointed not to find them.

━━

Inside, the chapel is almost monastic in its simplicity: whitewashed walls, plain glass in the windows, almost the only ornament a lovely della Robbia plaque of the Virgin and Child (given by Evelyn, who brought it from Italy) on the north wall. The chapel is silent, filled with slanting late afternoon light. I sit for a long time, rejoicing in the nourishing atmosphere one often finds in places much prayed in.

When the chapel was first dedicated in 1933, Evelyn noticed the same thing:

> All those who entered it for the first time on Friday were . . . impressed and surprised by the atmosphere of established spiritual peace. Perhaps the fact that the whole House and its garden have ever been for those who love and serve it, holy ground, may have something to do with the way in which this new expression of the inner life of Pleshey seems to have come into existence fully charged with the spirit of prayer, already offering to all who enter it "the silence of eternity interpreted by love."[17]

That last line, a quote from John Greenleaf Whittier, meant a great deal to Evelyn. She often compared the silence of eternity to the snowfields of the Alps—vast, remote, unbroken, compelling in their beauty and mystery:

> I remember once in the Alps finding myself alone in a high pasture surrounded by the strange almost unearthly mountain life. I was filled then with that absolute contentment and solemn happiness which hardly anything else can give to those who have the mountain sense. Above me I could only see the next bit of rough path, but on the other side of the valley I gazed at a great majestic range of snowy peaks and knew they were an earnest of what was above me—waiting for me too if only I would slog on, take a few risks—the hidden reason of the climb with all its hard work. . . .
>
> Now I think a Retreat should be rather like that: a pause when we can look across the valley and see the great spiritual snowfields in their beauty—Christ and the achievement of the Saints.[18]

I realize, sitting quietly in the chapel, watching the sunset light slide further up the white wall, that for a long time I have been aware only of "the next bit of rough path" in my life. I am glad I am here. It is good to climb to the high pastures sometimes, to see again the distant mountains toward which, by grace, our lives are leading—and in a sense, in which they already dwell.

As Evelyn Underhill would be quick to remind me, the spiritual life is not a matter of enjoying a pretty view or idly imagining living in an idyllic world; neither is it a question of determining what great distances of difficult terrain we can cover by our own efforts. Growth in prayer is growth into God, into Eternity. It is not a "case of our little souls standing face to face with the supernatural landscape external to us, and trying to get in touch with it by their own efforts; but rather of an ever-greater opening up of those souls in various ways and degrees to that spiritual reality in which they are already bathed, and by which they are already sustained and transfused."[19]

This "ever-greater opening up" of ourselves to God is of course the object of our lives, the ground and goal of all our prayer. But it is a difficult reality to grasp continuously, an arduous vocation to live out in the world—which is why periodic retreats to quiet havens like this one at Pleshey were so vital to Evelyn herself—and, I realize again, such a gift to me.

As the early darkness closes in, I leave the chapel in the shadows of the garden and return to the house. Upstairs again, after a pleasantly solitary supper in the refectory (at which I was happy to see—and eat—the fresh bread I had smelled on arrival), I discover, in a kind of cul-de-sac at the end of one of the corridors, a wooden door marked "Oratory." I open it and go in.

It is a tiny room, windowed on two sides but no larger than a closet. I kneel automatically on the prie-dieu in the center of the miniature space—there is physically no other place to put oneself—and find that I can extend my arms and touch the walls on either side. Ahead and to the left, windows give a view of the parish church and churchyard, and the bare trees against the last sunset light. A cross stands on the windowsill, and a Bible and the Book of Common Prayer on the small shelf of the kneeler. And that is all. But I don't know when I have encountered a space that felt more perfectly proportioned or furnished. I stay a long time in the tranquil embrace of the minute oratory, breathing in the pure air from the snowfields.

At bedtime I luxuriate in the emptiness of the house by making myself a mug of chamomile tea in the "buttery" on the landing and wandering the "upstairs indoors silences" in my dressing gown and slippers. At the other end of the same corridor that houses the oratory I discover the "conductor's room"—a small sitting room with a large window, just space enough for two comfortable chairs, a table, and a lamp. Here Evelyn would meet for individual conferences with retreatants, gently helping them to "open their souls to God," to breathe their "native air." I linger for a while, curled up in the retreatant's chair with my mug of tea, feeling the echoes of Evelyn's famous tranquillity, gentleness, and strength,[20] before I return to Charity and climb into bed.

In the morning, I rise early and pull open the heavy curtains by the window, standing for a moment to gaze at the chapel and the garden below. It is one of those quiet moments just before sunrise, when day and night seem balanced, when morning seems to hold its breath.

I had been disappointed, on arrival, to realize that I was at Pleshey at last but had missed—as one untimely born—the chance ever to experience a retreat under Evelyn Underhill's own gifted guidance. Now, I wonder. It makes me smile to think that, just perhaps—in the communion of saints and the fellowship of the Holy Spirit—the welcome of fresh bread and rose geraniums, the providential emptiness of the house, the general air of benediction, might be part of her careful, affectionate arrangements for yet another guest at Pleshey.

I hope so. In any event, I salute the new day—thanking God and Evelyn for the grace to hear, for a time, "the silence of Eternity interpreted by love"—and go downstairs to begin my retreat.

Coventry Cathedral ruins

Chapter 14

Coventry Cathedral

"Father forgive"

Given Coventry Cathedral's trial by fire in World War II and its postwar ministry of reconciliation, there are few better places to wrestle with forgiveness in our own lives.

—DAVID

I WALK INTO the bombed-out nave, its windows empty of stained glass, only its roofless sandstone walls revealing the medieval cathedral that crumpled under Nazi explosions.

A few yards away rises Coventry's new postwar cathedral, but I begin here in the ruined shell's sobering chill. On the night of November 14, 1940, Hermann Goering, commander-in-chief of the German Luftwaffe, unleashed nearly 450 bombers from bases in Brittany for the air raid on Coventry. Timed to the full moon and perversely code-named Operation Moonlight Sonata, the operation dropped five hundred tons of high explosives and forty thousand firebombs over eleven hours. It was the first attempt in history to destroy an entire city in a single air attack.

Coventry suffered enormously. The bombing killed or seriously injured over fourteen hundred people. Goering added a new word to the lexicon: other British cities, he warned, would soon be "coventrated."

One of the buildings destroyed was this cathedral, which traced its roots back to the twelfth century. The new cathedral could have been built over this same site instead of adjacent to it, but the architect resolved to retain these walls as a memorial. In the open air, with its tracery empty of glass, the ruined shell stretches toward the sky in perpetual Calvary.

The hum of traffic and smell of diesel drift through the old nave, hinting of the very industriousness that drew Nazi bombers in the first place to Coventry, the center of Britain's motor and aviation industry, one hundred miles northwest of London. The cathedral's losses were not unique; the building shared the fate of other portions of Coventry. Fire watchers had attempted to quench the incendiary bombs, but water and sand ran out and flames spread. With water trucks busy over the city, the men salvaged what they could as fire fed on the wooden pews, organ, and roof beams. It was "as though I were watching the crucifixion of Jesus upon his cross," Provost R. T. Howard recalled as he witnessed a place where Christians had worshiped for hundreds of years being destroyed in one night.[1]

The morning after the bombing, the cathedral's stonemason took two charred oaken beams from the debris and tied them together into a cross. Another man, a local Anglican priest, plucked from the ruins three medieval nails and fashioned them into a second cross. These two images became Coventry's postwar witness, symbols of both Good Friday and Easter. Physical destruction, the burnt crosses insisted, did not have the final word.

In the chill of an early December afternoon, I work my way slowly down the ruined nave. A charred cross, a replica of the original, surmounts the stone altar, its burnt blackness in startling contrast to the clean, polished wood of most church crosses.

A damp breeze blows through the roofless sanctuary. In the wall behind the altar, two words have been carved into the red sandstone, their letters a foot high: *FATHER FORGIVE*. Using Jesus' words from the cross, the provost chose to echo in stone the cathedral's postwar mission. Inscribed in the days following the bombing, they seem aimed both at the men flying the long-silenced planes and at contemporary consciences.

The prayer invokes not human aid but divine will. Interestingly, the petition includes only two words. By not adding the word *them*, another possible interpretation exists: "Father forgive us."

Coventry's message is a timely one for me, preoccupied with forgiveness as I have never been before. A church in my own life has been metaphorically shattered as destructively as Coventry; anger and distrust have explosively fragmented the worshiping community. Former friends have wielded the mandate to forgive like an ax in the confusion of who has committed wrong.

Perhaps in Coventry I would find hints of what forgiveness is and demands of us. It is not simply forgetting—the stark presence of the ruined shell prevents that. And as a posted sign in large letters reminds visitors, "Forgiveness Is Not Easy." But that only explains what forgiveness is not. I have a flash of anger. What right had the provost to order "Father forgive" inscribed? It is easy for a cathedral to forgive, for a provost who had not lost a child in the air raid. What about those families who suffered deaths and injuries? Disabled survivors still hobble through Coventry. Why extend forgiveness to bombers who were uncomprehending and unrepentant?

I think of the anger I feel myself for a church upheaval far away, for betrayal and falsehood, and nursing those grievances, I put off forgiveness till another time.

~

Shortly before visiting Coventry, while staying at a Scottish inn, I had encountered a white-haired tourist who praised Britain's cathedrals and extolled in particular the architectural drama of Coventry's new, postwar cathedral. Over our breakfast at a common table, I asked her what she thought of Coventry's emphasis on forgiveness.

I saw her stiffen as she cut into her eggs. In my sleepy state I belatedly realized that her accent was German. She paused before replying, then said evenly that Dresden, too, was wantonly firebombed. Forgiveness, she suggested, runs two ways, does it not? As if there were no original fault, no first blow thrown, she implied that bombings of

Coventry and Dresden canceled each other in equivalent blame. And we reached an impasse over our breakfast.

Before entering the new cathedral, I pass the former vestries, now an International Center rebuilt after the war, a sign explains, by young volunteers from Germany "making amends for suffering caused by their parents' generation." Coventry Cathedral, in its first project for reconciliation, helped construct the wing of a hospital in Germany. Its location: Dresden.

Leaving the ruins, I pass under the canopy that links the weathered red shell at a right angle to the modern sanctuary, built between 1954 and 1962 out of the same Staffordshire sandstone.

A clear glass screen, seventy feet high and etched with figures of angels, apostles, and prophets, serves as the new cathedral's transparent back wall. I peer through it into the lighted nave, a sanctuary offering warmth on a darkening winter afternoon. Architect Basil Spence wrote that his desire to design a cathedral stemmed from a wartime incident during D-Day in Normandy when he had witnessed the destruction of a beautiful church by tanks seeking to kill a German sniper. In postwar England, as a little-known architect, he had submitted his drawing for Coventry's open design competition without "the faintest hope of success."[2]

He received with amazement the news that he had won, later recounting in *Phoenix at Coventry:* "It was lunchtime but I felt I had to go to Saint Paul's Cathedral for a while. I went in and stayed under Christopher Wren's great dome quietly for about an hour. I felt a period of dedication was called for as I had a desperate need to be alone and to meditate quietly."[3]

The first British cathedral built since the Reformation received global publicity. The world peered over his shoulder to see what green shoots he could coax from the ashes.

Spence later recalled that in the postwar era of disillusionment, Sir David Eccles wrote to the mayor of Coventry, suggesting that "acts of faith" were more than ever needed to pierce the gloom. Spence adopted the phrase himself, viewing his design as a response to God. "The new Cathedral Church of Coventry," explained Spence, "is our Act of Faith."[4]

~~

Once inside, I step to a quiet corner in the back of the nave, out of the thin stream of tourists entering in the late afternoon. Ahead of me the cavernous sanctuary soars up to a vault of concrete and spruce slating. Except for slender tapering columns that support the roof, the cathedral's scale seems vast. Organ pipes on balconies ascend four stories while the tapestry behind the altar, reputed to be the world's largest at 72 feet by 38 feet, depicts the risen Christ on his throne.

I am vaguely conscious of the niches harboring Coventry's renowned works of art depicting biblical themes of justice and reconciliation. But I am unprepared for the floor-to-ceiling wall of stained glass to my right. Known as the Baptistry Window, it consists of hundreds of separate panels of blues, reds, and greens that surround a central orb of gradually lightening yellow panels. Even in the dusk of December, the window summons enough light to create the sensation of being lit from within.

Designer John Piper and glass builder Patrick Reyntiens intended to suggest the inbreaking of the Holy Spirit. The abstract pattern conjures up for me a long-buried dream of a mountainous Dantean ascent into light. I did not expect this beauty. I find myself suddenly seated in a pew, having been gently knocked off my feet by light.

I had arrived well in time for Saturday's choral evensong and planned to sit in one of the pews, but an usher directs me instead to the clergy stalls in the choir. To one side of me sits a white-haired, genial Anglican priest, and a name plate indicates that I occupy the bishop of Warwickshire's chair. My fellow parishioners number five, with the choir itself ten times that number. I revel in the intimacy of the gathering, awash in song, prayer, and silence, all under brilliant nave lights that keep the grey of the December afternoon at bay.

Benjamin Britten's *War Requiem* premiered here, shortly after the cathedral's consecration in 1962. The composer linked verses from World War I poet Wilfred Owen to the Latin Mass for the Dead, dedicating his work, in Owen's words, to "Whatever shares / The eternal reciprocity of tears."[5]

I look down the dark sanctuary, through its glass screen to the ruined shell of the medieval cathedral. In days following the bombing, the provost admitted that Christians in Coventry had agonized over how to respond to the hatred caused by the city's destruction. A number of possible options were open to the community. Citing a quote he attributed to C .S. Lewis, Provost Williams recalled, "The angels of God hold their breath to see which way we will choose to go."[6]

On the high altar, the crosses of nails and charred beams insist that sacrifice and pain occurred here once, only to be transfigured by God. It is not a message I easily embrace as I look out into the dusk of Coventry. My mind still slips into grudges, rehearsing ripostes, picking at memories like scabs trying to heal.

The bishop of Coventry had urged Basil Spence to design an altar and build a church around it. But the unremarkable black marble altar, dwarfed by the Graham Sutherland tapestry, seems to me the least imposing part of the new cathedral.

In part, the scale of other works draws the eye: the height of the nave, the luminous Baptistry Window that rises above a font of Palestinian limestone at its base, and the tapestry itself of Christ on the throne clothed in white robes.

My attention radiates out to pieces of artwork donated from around the world, each sculpture an act of faith in itself. The images seem less to decorate the cathedral than support it, clarifying biblical messages with tactile directness. There is the carved wooden Christ sunken in wood, given by a former Czech prisoner, as well as a metallic model of the city of Coventry set beneath an oversized, divinelike, plumb line. Startlingly impressive is a small chrome sculpture of a head of Christ, eyes closed, wearing a crown of thorns. The sculptor used metal from a car crash that took three lives. I had read of this particular work of art and expected to be repulsed by it. But I find instead that the sculpture, like the cross formed from the cathedral's charred roof beams, seems to convey an inexhaustible meaning: Nothing can separate us from Christ.

As he designed the cathedral, Basil Spence kept in mind the words, "Only the very best will do for God."[7] Two small chapels, projecting out into the world, encourage visitors to unite faith and work as Spence himself did.

The slender Chapel of Unity, built in the shape of a ten-sided crusader's tent, extends hope for all Christian denominations to be brought together by common prayer. The Chapel of Industry, composed of clear panes looking out on modern Coventry, attempts to shrink the distance between spirit and commerce in daily life.

Like the various sculptures, the chapels nudge visitors to consider how they themselves are to respond with "acts of faith." I look out the glass at the city's evening traffic. Is forgiveness, I ask myself, an act of faith?

The cathedral's ministry extends far into the world. For decades it sponsored an international network of people devoted to reconciliation. Under the rubric of the Cross of Nails Ministry, participants sought to pray, teach, and fund-raise on behalf of projects aiming to reduce conflict in Northern Ireland, South Africa, the Middle East, and Europe. Members met in small gatherings, often committing themselves to a simpler way of life. Active chapters evolved in several countries, notably the United States and Germany, with the U.K. branch of the Cross of Nails Ministry eventually superseded by mission efforts of Coventry Cathedral itself.

"The Ministry helped people to come to terms with their enemies and to see a mirror image of themselves in their enemies," says the Reverend Canon Paul Oestreicher, the cathedral's former director of international ministry. Like Coventry itself, Oestreicher's experience with forgiveness transcended the abstract. "My father was Jewish," he explains, "and relatives died in Auschwitz. I had to come to terms with forgiving the German people." Oestreicher chronicles part of that passage in his book *The Double Cross*, whose pages "focus on 'the love that will not let me go.'"[8]

～

I spend Saturday evening outside the cathedral, walking nearly deserted downtown streets of Coventry where Lady Godiva once rode—presumably in a warmer month than December—trying to persuade her nobleman husband to lower his subjects' taxes. Much of the city's current architecture stands in dispiriting contrast with its cathedral. Bleak concrete boxes rise as testament not only to postwar reconstruction but prewar urban planning that demolished much of Coventry's medieval charm.

After a supper of fish and chips in a nearby restaurant, I return to my small bed-and-breakfast, a fifteen-minute walk from the cathedral, just beyond where bombs fell in November 1940, and sleep restlessly.

Early Sunday morning I return to the cathedral, entering the small Chapel of Christ in Gethsemane through a wrought-iron gate shaped like a crown of thorns. On the wall ahead, a dazzling bronze relief represents a kneeling angel offering the chalice in the garden of Gethsemane.

Only a handful of people attend this service of morning prayer. In the stillness of the chapel, several thoughts accompany me. It seems that we avoid extending forgiveness for several reasons: first, we worry that we may be opening floodgates, acceding to future injury poured in upon past wrong (although, as C. S. Lewis noted, "there is all the difference in the world between forgiving and excusing"[9]); and second, less commendably, we must surrender outrage. Guarding grudges like heirlooms, we demand retribution and vindication.

And then, of course, there is memory. The contemporary slogan "Remember and forgive" has modified the ancient axiom "Forgive and forget." And yet, if there exists a room of forgiveness that I occasionally enter, memory seems to open under me like a trap door.

"It is impossible to forgive unless we recognize our own need for forgiveness," suggests Bruderhof pastor Johann Christoph Arnold, "and acknowledge our faults to someone else."[10] In words often credited to the priest and poet George Herbert, "He that cannot forgive others breaks the bridge over which he himself must pass if he would ever reach heaven; for everyone has need to be forgiven."

Ultimately, the breathed prayer "Father forgive" may become "Father forgive . . . me." After the flurry of outrage and accusation, we pause, no less convinced that others have committed wrong, yet down on our own knees in penance.

~

The choir prepares to process for the Sunday morning Eucharist, past chairs that could seat a thousand people, yet the sanctuary is barely a quarter filled. As the cathedral's provost waits in line to begin the processional, I talk with him. He welcomes me and speaks briefly of his earlier predecessor who had ordered the words *Father Forgive* engraved.

"Many people seriously criticized him for his call to forgiveness," he admits. We agree that his was a brave response. Visionary as well, he adds, "and terribly difficult."

Huge stone tablets, eight in all, line the sides of the nave. They are engraved, a brochure notes, with "the most profound words spoken by Christ," like verbal stations of the cross. I stand under one that begins, "Come unto me, all ye that labour and are heavy laden, and I will give you rest," briefly considering what I would excerpt for such tablets.

Words that have been on my mind (yet curiously absent from these tablets) come from Matthew 6:14-15: "For if you forgive others their trespasses, your heavenly Father will also forgive you; but if you do not forgive others, neither will your Father forgive your trespasses." C. S. Lewis insisted unequivocally, "There is no doubt about the second part of this statement. It is in the Lord's Prayer: it was emphatically stated by our Lord. If you don't forgive you will not be forgiven. No part of his teaching is clearer: and there are no exceptions to it."[11] I think of the parable of the unforgiving servant. I hear a harshness to the words, and a terrible truth colors the parable for those of us who have been forgiven much and who forgive little.

"There is a hard law," noted Alan Paton, "that when a deep injury is done to us, we never recover until we forgive."[12] I have tended to think of forgiveness parsimoniously, as if it were a gift to withhold from others. But here in Coventry, forgiveness strikes me more along the lines of a key, given to us by God to open a prison cell locked from inside.

I have a train to catch in a few hours, but before leaving, I climb the surviving steeple of the ruined church, up its 180 winding steps to a parapet that looks out over the grey urban sea of Coventry.

The spire is the third highest in Britain, and from this crow's nest it is possible to see for miles in all directions. There are few points of the compass where the cathedral's role as reconciler has not been felt—in Africa, Asia, Latin America, and Europe, most notably in Germany itself.

Before Paul Oestreicher's retirement as the cathedral's international director, the German government honored him for his work in Anglo-German relations. "Through no other sustained aspect of my ministry," he writes in *The Double Cross,* "could I better demonstrate to myself and to others my understanding of reconciliation and peace." He speaks now of the "prayer and inner process" that allowed him to forgive, adding, "I wasn't a free human being until I came to terms with forgiving the German people."[13]

Corrie ten Boom, author of *The Hiding Place,* writes of an incident in Munich after the war. On a lecture tour during which she had preached of the need for forgiveness, she was confronted by a "beaming and bowing" former S. S. jailer of Ravensbruck prison, where her beloved sister perished and she herself barely survived. After the man stretched out his hand, she tried to raise her own hand and could not.

> I felt nothing, not the slightest spark of warmth or charity. And so again I breathed a silent prayer. *Jesus, I cannot forgive him. Give me Your forgiveness.*
>
> As I took his hand the most incredible thing happened. From my shoulder along my arm and through my hand a current seemed to pass

from me to him, while into my heart sprang a love for this stranger that almost overwhelmed me.

And so I discovered that it is not on our forgiveness any more than on our goodness that the world's healing hinges, but on His. When He tells us to love our enemies, He gives, along with the command, the love itself.[14]

The wind buffets me as I stand in the tower's parapet. Querulously, I pick at the fringes of her story, troubled by the image of a "beaming and bowing" guard. Was that contrition? But the guard's demeanor is not her point (and in any case, as writer and teacher Kyle Pasewark suggests, "Repentance is a response to forgiveness, not its condition").[15]

As practiced by men and women like Paul Oestreicher and Corrie ten Boom—and by places like Coventry Cathedral—forgiveness mutes the objections of bystanders. And perhaps this is a quality of forgiveness. We depend on others who have suffered more deeply to show us the way out of the debris of anger.

⸺

From the steeple on this overcast Sunday morning, I take a last view down into the old cathedral, where a few figures move about lost in thought. At noon this coming Friday, and every Friday ("in sun and pouring rain, with two people present or fifty," notes a canon), visitors will gather around the altar in the roofless nave for a short service that begins with the Coventry Litany of Reconciliation.

"All have sinned and fallen short of the glory of God," the prayer begins before traversing a confession of the seven deadly sins. Uttered simultaneously at noon on Fridays throughout the world in conflicted settings, the litany ends with another echo from the apostle Paul, quoted as well on signs in the new cathedral: "Be kind to one another, tender-hearted, forgiving one another, as God in Christ forgave you."

In all Britain there is perhaps no better setting than Coventry to reckon with forgiveness. Yet if the power to forgive comes from God, our ability to forgive begins with prayer. And that can begin anywhere.

In Coventry we confront the paradox that we have postponed what we profess to pray for each day: ". . . as we forgive those who trespass against us." A tenacious wind carries up the sound of traffic from streets far below. It is time to descend the steeple steps and return home.

Addison's Walk, Magdalen College, Oxford

Chapter 15

Oxford and C. S. Lewis

"The deepest thirst within us"

Historic Oxford (like the past and like life itself) is mysteriously full of doors. Even if the ones you want seem closed to you at first, keep hoping and trying: there is generally another way in.

—DEBORAH

I AM ON THE OUTSIDE, looking in. And the porter is on to me: twice now I have tried, under cover of the lawful entry of Oxford dons, to slip past the watchful old dragon and attain the sacred precincts of Magdalen College. Each time, however, he has pounced and stopped me, triumphantly reminding me what a placard has already largely declared: The College Is Closed to All Visitors. "We are resurfacing," the porter announces importantly, although what that might mean baffles me. The tantalizing glimpses through the gateway of stone walls, grassy quad, quiet flower beds, and neat paths all reveal perfectly adequate surfaces, as far as I can see.

I explain that I have come a long way to pay homage to one of the college's most eminent fellows, C. S. Lewis, and that I merely want the most reverent, brief, and noninvasive of visits to Addison's Walk (the site of a starlit epiphany in Lewis's conversion to Christianity).

"Addison's Walk, is it?" the porter sniffs indignantly. "That's part of the Fellows' Garden, miss. You'd never be allowed in there in any event."

I have come so far and am now so near that I can hardly bear it that the way is closed to me. However, as at many other difficult moments

169

in my life, I draw strength from recalling a passage in one of Lewis's *Chronicles of Narnia.*

At the beginning of *The Silver Chair,* Jill and Eustace are desperately trying to find a way out of their school grounds, away from the bullies who are chasing them. They long for the peace and freedom of the open country that lies beyond the school wall.

> "If only the door was open again!" said Scrubb as they went on, and Jill nodded. For at the top of the shrubbery was a high stone wall, and in that wall a door by which you could get out onto open moor. This door was nearly always locked. But there had been times when people had found it open; or perhaps there had been only one time. But you may imagine how the memory of even one time kept people hoping, and trying the door.[1]

Taking courage from the example of Jill and Eustace, I am determined to keep "hoping, and trying the door." I retreat from the college gate to rethink my approach. There must be another way in: even in Narnia, the wardrobe wasn't the only door.

The narrow Oxford streets have been noisy and crowded with the perennial tourists and flurries of newly arrived undergraduates; exhaust from enormous buses fouls the air. I am grateful for the leafy quiet of the Angel Meadow just on the other side of Magdalen Bridge. From here, on the far side of the Cherwell as it slides by, I can see into the famous, frustratingly near, Magdalen College deer park. Just beyond, I know, is Addison's Walk, where on a fateful night in the fall of 1931 Lewis strolled with his friends J. R. R. Tolkien and Hugo Dyson, and somehow in the course of their conversation came finally to believe that Christianity was true.

Also on the far side of the river, beyond the barred gate, are Lewis's own suite of college rooms, the hall where he ate, the chapel where he prayed. All as inaccessible to me as if they were on the moon. I walk a long way down the river bank, seeking a way across—a bridge, a boat, stepping-stones, anything—but finally, as the afternoon light begins to fade, so does my hope. When Jill and Eustace reached the door in the wall, it was, by the grace of Aslan, unlocked, and opened into Narnia itself. But it seems I am to be shut out of Magdalen after all. Forlorn and disappointed, I acknowledge my exile.

Gradually however, I begin to notice the wind whispering in the magnificent old horse chestnut trees that tower and branch overhead like cathedral vaulting. I remember that when Lewis recalled that momentous night's conversation, he spoke of wind in trees just like these, a stone's throw away on the other side of the Cherwell: "A rush of wind which came so suddenly on the still, warm evening and sent so many leaves pattering down that we thought it was raining. We held our breath."[2] Now I too catch my breath, remembering his memory as if it were my own, feeling the mystery of that long-past night breathe on my face. Suddenly C. S. Lewis, whose books have always fed and shaped my faith, feels very near at hand, the powerful freedom of that rushing wind as close as the breath in my lungs. Perhaps the reality of that epiphany is not so remote as I had thought.

There usually is, as an old friend of Narnia ought to have remembered, more than one way in.

On the path in front of me, windfall horse chestnuts—called "conkers"—shine darkly from among the fallen leaves, and I am further comforted. "Buckeyes" we called them when I was a child, and would gather them on autumn walks with my beloved Ohio grandmother. Impulsively I pick one up and put it in my pocket. Its smooth roundness reassures me as I close my hand around it.

—

The complicated sensations of that moment under the wind-murmuring trees on the banks of the river—part heart-lifting awe, part piercing sadness, memory entwined with longing and with love—Lewis himself knew well. He called it Joy. It would be difficult to exaggerate the importance of this recurrent experience of Joy for Lewis. In his spiritual autobiography, significantly titled *Surprised by Joy*, he claims that "in a sense the central story of my life is about nothing else."[3]

Lewis carefully distinguished Joy from Pleasure or Happiness. Joy is a sharp desire, a mystical longing both painful and sweet—a kind of spiritual homesickness for a home we scarcely remember. Joy is, as Lewis's friend Tolkien explained it, "a sudden and miraculous grace . . . beyond the walls of the world, poignant as grief."[4] The elusive link with memory is key: the first time Lewis experienced Joy was "itself the memory of a memory"—the fragrance of a flowering currant bush reminded him suddenly of a toy garden his older brother Warren had created with moss and twigs in the lid of a biscuit tin and brought into the nursery when Lewis was about four years old.[5]

Lewis eventually came to realize that his experience of Joy was essentially mystical—an experience of the natural world as revelation of the goodness and love of God. The memory of that toy garden made him "aware of nature . . . as something cool, dewy, fresh, exuberant." It was "the first beauty I ever knew"—and he knew it as a message from a far country. It awakened within him a profound longing for the source of that beauty: "As long as I live my imagination of Paradise will retain something of my brother's toy garden."[6]

Warren (called Warnie) and Lewis (called Jack) remained close friends all their lives. "We were allies, not to say confederates, from the first," Lewis wrote.[7] After the death of their mother when Jack was nine, the bereft brothers came "to rely more and more exclusively on each other for all that made life bearable; to have confidence only in each other."[8] It is easy to imagine the brothers in an autumn wood like this Oxford one, companionably gathering conkers in the time-honored schoolboy manner. With an obscure but haunting gratitude for all our childhoods—theirs, and mine, and those of all the children in Narnia— I firmly grip the conker in my pocket and turn around, to cross the bridge and head back to town.

It is dusk when I regain the High Street; the shops are closing, the college bells beginning to toll six o'clock. Remembering the summer I spent in Oxford in my own student days, and the refreshment of sung evensong at Christ Church, I impulsively turn left at St. Aldgates and find a seat in the choir of the tiny, nearly empty Christ Church Cathedral.

As I kneel to pray I notice on the narrow shelf directly in front of me, gleaming auburn in the dim light, a perfect horse chestnut. A beauty

of a conker, twin to the one from the trees by the river. I accept it gratefully and tuck it with the other inside my jacket pocket.

Ironically, I was possibly closer to Lewis in that sense of exile—the
painful consciousness of being excluded from some marvelous reality
just on the other side of a closed door—than I might have been if the
porter had allowed me the longed-for glimpse of Addison's Walk.
Images of doors, gates, magical entries, abound in Lewis's writing, testimony to his own "longing to be on the inside of some door which
we have always seen from the outside.[9] There is indeed perhaps no more
characteristic—nor more valuable—insight from Lewis's entire canon
than his deep awareness that we are, all our mortal lives, far from our
real home. He reminds us that we long to return, that "the deepest thirst
within [us is] not adapted to the deepest nature of the world."[10] As he
reasoned, "If I find in myself a desire which no experience in this world
can satisfy, the most probable explanation is that I was made for another world."[11]

This "lifelong nostalgia, our longing to be reunited with something
in the universe from which we now feel cut off" is, Lewis insisted, "the
truest index of our real situation"[12] and in fact one of the best things
about our pilgrim human state. "Our best havings are wantings," as
Lewis wrote to a friend.[13] Psyche realizes in Lewis's novel *Till We Have
Faces* that "the sweetest thing in all my life has been the longing to find
the place where all the beauty came from."[14] These inconsolable longings are a kind of homing device, placed in our hearts by grace. Joy is
sweet, even in its knife-edged sadness, because it is a gift from God,
who longs, beyond all our imaginings, to draw us to himself.

Throughout the Narnia Chronicles, Lewis infuses his characters'
adventures with experiences of Joy. In these moments, consistent with
his own experience as a child, memories of earlier times in Narnia and
a yearning to return—and especially to meet Aslan again—are key. In
a lyrical passage at the end of *The Lion, the Witch and the Wardrobe*,
Lewis assumes his readers also have shared this piercing longing, and

makes a direct appeal to that memory. After many adventures, Aslan and the children finally reach the castle of Cair Paravel on its little hill by the sea:

> Before them were the sands, with rocks and little pools of salt water, and seaweed, and the smell of the sea and long miles of bluish-green waves breaking for ever and ever on the beach. And oh, the cry of the sea-gulls! Have you heard it? Can you remember?[15]

About three miles from the center of Oxford is the village of Headington Quarry, on the outskirts of which Jack and Warnie shared a rambling brick house, called the Kilns. Lewis also had his rooms in college, of course, where he met with students for tutorials and gathered with his friends, but the Kilns was really his home from 1930 until his death in 1963.[16]

Remembering my thwarted efforts to get into Magdalen College, I was careful not to assume that I would be allowed to enter the hallowed precincts of the Kilns, now privately owned. Nevertheless, the following morning I boarded the Headington bus, as Lewis (who never learned to drive a car) habitually did for decades.

The bus ride itself is part of the pilgrims' route: Lewis records a decisive moment in his long journey toward Christian faith that occurred on the top of a Headington bus—a moment that had everything to do with doorways into other worlds, with finally saying yes to the invitations of God.

> I was going up Headington Hill on the top of a bus. . . . I became aware that I was holding something at bay, or shutting something out. . . . I felt myself being, there and then, given a free choice. I could open the door or keep it shut. . . . I knew that to open the door . . . meant the incalculable. . . . I chose to open. . . . Enough had been thought, and said, and felt, and imagined. It was about time that something should be done.[17]

Lewis had, after long toying with philosophical and intellectual constructs of Christianity, come to the crossroads. He recognized that a "wholly new situation" had developed: "I was to be allowed to play at philosophy no longer. . . . Total surrender, the absolute leap in the dark, were demanded."[18]

Getting off the bus at Risinghurst, the stop beyond Headington Quarry, I ask my way, street by street, from young women with babies in prams and old men with garden rakes, and eventually find a small sign indicating the entrance to the Kilns. It is a handsome two-story house of mellow brick, set in lovely gardens, still ablaze with late flowers, sheltering under grand old trees.

With some trepidation I knock on the side door (neatly marked "Tradesmen's Entrance," which I doubt it was when Lewis lived there), and explain my errand to the pleasant young Englishwoman who opens it. She is a recently qualified physician, a tenant-cum-caretaker at the Kilns, which has been purchased by an American organization to be a kind of Lewis study-and-conference-center. Despite the early hour and despite having herself no particular interest in C. S. Lewis, she courteously offers to show me around. I am grateful for the chance to see inside the carefully "restored" house, which is far more attractive than I had imagined somehow, but the general ambience is flat: there is no mystery (and not much reality) here.

Frankly bewildered by the extravagant reverence paid the house by her landlords, my guide points out the ceiling of the study, once stained yellow with smoke from countless Lewisian pipes: it has been carefully painted over, and then expensively repainted to resemble a smoke-stained ceiling.

Upstairs, in the bedroom where Lewis slept for many years and where he died, I am suddenly both moved and embarrassed. I admit my own discomfort at trespassing on such intimate space. The young woman nods sympathetically. "One wonders how he would feel," she agrees. "Surely he would rather people simply read his books and left it at that."

Holy Trinity Church, the rural-feeling Anglican parish where Jack and Warren Lewis worshiped, is a short walk from the Kilns, and a glorious one on this fine October morning. The Lewis brothers loved these woods, especially in autumn, with "its still, windless days . . . and all the yellow leaves still on the trees."[19] The small stone church is set in a tranquil churchyard with flagged paths winding among ancient yew trees and lichen-covered gravestones. It is difficult to believe that the noise and congestion of Oxford are so close. This place might be deep in the peaceful countryside.

Once again I encounter a locked door, but this time I am not about to be turned away. The young rector, whom I find at the rectory next door, cheerfully lends me his own key, and for an hour I am completely alone in the church. Rarely, however, has my solitude been so richly companioned.

About halfway down the side aisle on the north side, a discreet brass plaque marks the pew where the Lewis brothers invariably sat together on Sunday mornings. It is a small pew, only big enough for two, as one of the stone pillars interrupts at that point, conveniently separating the brothers from their neighbors, and sheltering them from view. I sit there myself for a long time, praying with and for them—two bulky middle-aged men in tweeds and flannels, reclusive and protective of each other.

Poignantly the window nearest the abbreviated pew is a memorial window to two other brothers, boys in the parish who died young. It would be striking anywhere. Made not of traditional stained glass but of clear glass delicately engraved, it creates shifting effects of light and shadow through which the trees and sky can be half-seen. Moving closer to examine the etching, my heart lifts to recognize scenes from all of Narnia—there is Aslan himself, radiant as the sun, and the lamppost and the valiant little *Dawn Treader*—there is Jill riding on the back of Glimfeather the owl. There is Reepicheep, and all the talking beasts, and the trees and mountains and rivers of a country I have known and loved since I was ten. My own true country in my childhood, which I would have entered without hesitation at any moment of my life if any actual way had ever opened to me, and which in fact I inhabit still, still claim as homeland, in the imagination of my heart.

C. S. Lewis always remembered vividly the frosty October evening at a train station bookstall when he picked up a used copy of *Phantastes* by George MacDonald, a book through which "the wind of Joy" blew continuously. "That night my imagination was . . . baptized," he realized.[20] Lewis's own Narnia Chronicles baptized mine; it was he who taught me to lift my face to those mysterious winds, to love and to seek my own true country.

—

Lewis spoke once (at evensong, at the Oxford University Church of St. Mary the Virgin) about Joy, about the sense of exile that seems inseparable from our perception of beauty, about our "desire for our own far-off country, which we find in ourselves even now":

> We do not want merely to *see* beauty . . . we want . . . to be united with the beauty we see, to pass into it, to receive it into ourselves, . . . to become part of it.

Lewis went on to assure his audience that this longing will not go forever unsatisfied:

> At present we are on the outside of the world, the wrong side of the door. We discern the freshness and purity of morning, but they do not make us fresh and pure. We cannot mingle with the splendours we see. But all the leaves of the New Testament are rustling with the rumour that it will not always be so. Some day, God willing, we shall get *in*.[21]

Decades before I read that lyrical promise, I had already encountered its truth in Narnia. In *The Silver Chair* (in what remains one of my favorite passages), the children, who have been held as prisoners in the dark Underworld, escape from the evil queen and begin to attempt their way out of darkness.

Finally they come to a hole high on the wall of the tunnel in which they are traveling, a hole through which shines a pale blue light. Jill climbs up and through the hole—and finds herself in Narnia again at last. She finds herself, in fact, emerging high on a moonlit hillside in the middle of a midwinter night. She is watching the Great Snow Dance, "which is done every year in Narnia on the first moonlit night when there is snow on the ground," in which a circle of dancing Fauns and Dryads is enclosed within a ring of Dwarfs circling in the opposite direction, skillfully throwing snowballs in between the dancers.

> They were throwing them through the dance in such perfect time with the music and with such perfect aim that if all the dancers were in exactly the right place at exactly the right moments, no one would be hit. . . . On fine nights when the cold and the drum-taps, and the hooting of the owls, and the moonlight, have got into their wild woodland blood and made it even wilder, they will dance till daybreak. I wish you could see it for yourselves.[22]

This moment of emergence and recognition is, in its own Narnian way, a beatific vision of redemption. "They had not only got out into the Upper World at last, but had come out in the heart of Narnia. Jill felt she could have fainted with delight." Knowing that their deliverance has been accomplished, that their long captivity is over, Jill turns to shout down to the others, "I say! It's all right. We're out, and we're home."[23]

I have one more thing to do before I leave the churchyard. It does not take long to find the grave; small arrows on low signs show the way. The Lewis brothers are buried together under a flat granite stone (almost exactly the size and shape of a large door). The brothers' names and the dates of their lives are carved in the lower half of the stone; the upper half is occupied by a deeply incised cross. I stand at the foot of the grave for a long time, unexpectedly overwhelmed by an awareness of all I owe to Lewis, my lifelong teacher and guide. I am brimful of awe and gratitude, love and sorrow, memory and desire: a joy, in fact, as poignant as grief. I wish, suddenly, that I had thought to bring flowers; I long to make some kind of offering.

The sun is bright, making dancing shadows on the dappled ground, but the wind is cold, scattering leaves over the stone. I push my hands into my jacket pockets and find the two conkers I put there the day before. Impulsively I bring them out to lay on the grave and, kneeling, discover that once again someone has been there before me: at the center of the cross, so deeply tucked into the space that I had not noticed it before, another perfect conker rests.

I add my two, making a burnished trinity of childish homage.

It is deeply good to know that "it's all right"—that Lewis, like Jill and the others, has "got in." Thanks be to God, Jack and Warren Lewis are, as we all shall be someday, safely and forever on the far side of the door, inside at last. At home.

The chapel at Little Gidding

Chapter 16

Little Gidding and Nicholas Ferrar & T. S. Eliot

"To kneel where prayer has been valid"

Little Gidding rests at a crossroads for poets, kings, and pilgrims. Visitors return here, to T. S. Eliot's "intersection of the timeless moment," to be reminded of the possibility of living everywhere at the same juncture.

—DAVID

I AWAKEN EARLY at Little Gidding. Rising on one elbow, I watch as mist slowly thins outside our window to reveal a steeple. Deborah is awake as well. She steps lightly across the creaking floor of the nineteenth-century farmhouse.

We have traveled across much of Britain over the years, and it seems appropriate to wake up together here this March morning, her birthday, near the very center of England. I join her at our bedroom window. Across the lawn barely a stone's throw away, Little Gidding's chapel—a literary beacon and a way station for pilgrims—emerges from the grey dawn.

Long before I knew it existed as a place, I had heard of Little Gidding as a poem by T. S. Eliot (1888–1965), the last of his *Four Quartets*, written from the ashes of World War II and reflective of Eliot's own wobbly journey of faith. "A muted longing for renewal breathes through the opening of the last *Quartet*," observes Lyndall Gordon in her keen-eyed biography of Eliot. "This life . . . always has a single aim:

to recover the divine."[1] I had only glimmerings at first of the poem's "literal, moral, and mystical" layers of meaning,[2] but I found its verses were like rough map coordinates leading to a far country. Eliot seemed to have caught sight of a luminous region from which he dispatched reassurance of God's love. "Little Gidding" was the most comforting poem I knew.

One of the world's most renowned poems took its title from one of Britain's most obscure sites. An American friend once sought out this enclave of chapel and farm buildings, unmarked on all but the most detailed maps. Noting its unremarkable setting, tucked in a swell of barley fields at the end of a lane, he wondered whether Eliot had chosen it in part for that very reason. Unlike spectacular religious sites soaring out of granite outcrop or Gothic stone, this place rests in humble terrain. Little Gidding reminds visitors that any landscape, however ordinary, can draw one's breath toward prayer.

In the upstairs kitchen set aside for guests, Deborah and I make a breakfast of toast, cereal, and coffee. An overcast sky deepens the green of the fields outside the window. Most of our married life we have lived under the dazzling sun of New Mexico, where any rain falls as a blessing and grass passes like a zephyr, so the subtle green and grey of Great Britain never fails to delight us.

Though we are only a few miles from the A-1 Motorway, the damp air also filters out most sounds. "You won't find too many parts of England this quiet," the caretakers of Little Gidding, a genial, hospitable couple in their sixties, reminded us last night on our arrival.

The sprawling farmhouse shelters no other overnight guests, but Deborah and I talk quietly in the kitchen as we recall what attracted Eliot to Little Gidding in the first place. The Anglican deacon Nicholas Ferrar (1592–1637) founded a lay community here in 1626 noted for its life of prayer, work, and simplicity. The men and women ran a school, restored the chapel, and gathered three times a day for worship, using the Book of Common Prayer. In this pastoral nook seventy-five miles north of London, they sheltered the fugitive King Charles I during the English civil war and suffered reprisals by Oliver Cromwell's troops.

The community lasted nearly three decades and provided Eliot (who visited here May 19, 1936) with "a distant paradigm of the contemplative life."[3] Jotting preliminary notes for his poem the day he visited Little Gidding, Eliot ended with this reflection: "Invocation to the Holy Spirit."[4] During the centuries that followed Ferrar's prayerful experiment, travelers occasionally made their way here. But for many visitors like myself, the poem "Little Gidding" charted the directions.

Deborah and I finish breakfast, wash dishes, then step outside into the spring morning. She crosses the wet grass to enter the chapel, while I head up the lane for a walk.

Reaching the top of the pasture, I turn and look behind me. The incline, slight as it is, allows a good view of farm buildings and fields beyond. The perspective also stirs a memory of the first time I saw Little Gidding years ago, driving alone down this lane to a place where history, poetry, and faith intersected.

⌐⌐

I came originally for a brief retreat on a December afternoon. I traveled by train, first to the city of Peterborough, then in a rented car along the congested A-1 Motorway. An exit ramp at last discharged me into the English countryside, and within minutes a pastoral hush descended like a quilt. I followed narrow roads to the village of Great Gidding, then past my turn until rerouted by an elderly pedestrian walking her dog. ("You missed the signpost to Little Gidding back near the pub, dear.") Another mile past fallow fields of rich black soil brought me to this lane.

Nicholas Ferrar's community had dispersed long before, but Little Gidding was home that December to a second Christian community that had come together during the last quarter of the twentieth century, prompted both by Ferrar's legacy of holy living and Eliot's incandescent poem. They welcomed retreatants as part of their ministry.

I carried with me notebooks to fill with firsthand images: the chapel where Ferrar's community had worshiped and Cromwell's troops rampaged; the setting immortalized by Eliot in *Four Quartets;* the farmhouse where the contemporary community gathered for prayer.

When I arrived that winter day, a robust, genial man in his mid-forties greeted me as he spread gravel for a new parking lot. He introduced himself as a member of Little Gidding's community, at the time numbering some fourteen people. The guestmaster, a thin, ex-military mechanic, soon joined us. He took me on a brief tour of the farmhouse, pointing out its prayer room and parlor and noting its construction: "Essentially it's Victorian with pieces of Tudor brick floating around from Ferrar's manor house that burned."

Declining his offer of tea, I explained I wanted to see the chapel before dark. A low, copper-colored winter sun shed little light and even less heat as I walked across the lawn, carrying fragments of "Little Gidding" in my mind like pieces of pottery to reassemble here. I paused at the chapel's entrance and in the silence watched landmarks from Eliot's poem fall into place:

> . . . when you leave the rough road
> And turn behind the pig-sty to the dull façade
> And the tombstone.[5]

I had left the "rough road" (now paved) and turned at "the pig-sty" (since converted to sheds). I stood before the "dull façade"—the brick chapel's stone front—and saw that the tabletop "tombstone" in the walkway revealed Ferrar's own burial ground.

In this setting famed for community, I was alone. I pushed open the heavy wooden door, unable to resist reciting Eliot's verse:

> . . . So, while the light fails
> On a winter's afternoon, in a secluded chapel . . . [6]

I stepped into the small nave. Fading light from the altar window revealed paneled walls and a well-trodden floor of black and white marble. Nicholas Ferrar's seventeenth-century community—an extended family of his mother, brother, in-laws, and children—gathered daily for prayers here, facing one another on benches so close they could have touched across the narrow aisle. By stretching out my gloved hands, I could reach half the chapel's width.

There was more to chronicle, and at first I wrote it all down as though I were an insurance adjuster: brasses and memorials, glass windows and a fifteenth-century brass eagle lectern.

On the walls, several embroidered plaques displayed verses not only from Eliot but Ferrar's friend, George Herbert. (Though based in Bemerton, the poet and priest received income from the Leighton Bromswold church near Little Gidding and bequeathed to Ferrar his trove of poems.)

I picked up the visitors' book, but its signatures proved nearly illegible in the dusk. As I lowered myself onto a bench, weariness of the journey settled over me like road dust, and I glanced at the excerpt from "Little Gidding" framed on the chapel's wall:

> You are not here to verify,
> Instruct yourself, or inform curiosity
> Or carry report. You are here to kneel
> Where prayer has been valid.[7]

This was the verse Deborah and I had consulted like a compass throughout our travels in Britain. Eliot's injunction had disarmed many a tourist of notebook and pen. After several minutes I relinquished my own and rose from the bench. In the last light of day, I approached the altar rails and followed Eliot's advice.

Little Gidding was in darkness by the time I returned to the farm-house's large kitchen. Members of the community had made their way from work to tea and greeted me cordially as I joined with the current of their day. A kind-eyed octogenarian, one of the first to join in the late 1970s, listed the various religious traditions represented: "We have Quakers, Roman Catholics, Free Church, and Anglicans, but," she added with regret, "we don't have any Baptists."

In the hours that followed, I met most of the community. Some participants farmed the fields; others crafted furniture or held jobs in nearby towns, returning nightly to the small cluster of restored brick homes around the farmyard.

The men and women seemed not only of widely disparate ages but also temperaments, reminding me of the final scene in the movie *Places in the Heart* where characters separated by race and class (indeed by life and death) are reunited in the pews of a West Texas church during Communion.

As though tuning in on a family dialogue, I listened at the kitchen table to fast-paced exchanges laced with humor. At times banter seemed forced, hinting at the strain of close living. I would later learn of minor conflicts and quarrels; the original seventeenth-century experiment was not without its own.

Like Christian communities from Scotland's Iona to France's Taizé, the men and women had published their own devotional guide, *The Little Gidding Prayer Book,* offering to readers "both the daily worship of this motley band of people, and also its simple rule of life."[8]

The community's founder, Cambridge lecturer and Anglican priest Robert Van de Weyer, explained in *Little Gidding: Story and Guide:* "Our intention was always that people should come simply because they felt called to community life, and that we should support each other, materially and spiritually, in our various vocations."[9]

Nicholas Ferrar's household had oriented itself around daily prayer, and this latter-day community anchored itself similarly, meeting each morning in the farmhouse. Ferrar had excelled in London's commercial world before exchanging its premises for Little Gidding. His spiritual descendants in this current joint venture were themselves like investors, staking their life holdings for invisible dividends.

After dinner with the guestmaster, I took an upstairs bedroom in the farmhouse, its low ceiling humbling my six-foot-six frame. Though only a visitor on retreat, I felt an undeniable attraction to this way of life, with its balance of work, worship, and rest. I saw here pastoral lives with labor defined, a place where haste deferred to prayer. Moreover, the gathering itself—with companions to rein in wayward instincts—provided a certain accountability. "Our different strengths and insights complement one another," noted Van de Weyer, "so in our unity we can guide and sustain each other."[10]

Turning off my light, I looked out into the winter dark. Where was the spiritual community in my own life to gird and challenge me? Was it my local church congregation alone? I had at times skated out on community only to feel it crack under the weight of my trust. At other times, mistaking congeniality for community, I had gathered in pews more to enjoy those around me than to worship God, "led astray," as the Anglican writer Brigid Herman warned, by "confounding vital corporateness with mere gregariousness."[11] Yet Jesus' scriptural promise remained clear: "For where two or three are gathered in my name, I am there among them" (Matt. 18:20). As Brigid Herman also insisted: "We are in sober truth members one of another, and it is only in fellowship that we can realize God's purpose."[12]

I went to sleep that December night listening from my upstairs bedroom as members of the Little Gidding Community drifted back to their homes across the farmyard, calling to each other companionably in the icy air.

In the years following that initial stay, I tracked the community's course, but each time I telephoned or visited there seemed to be fewer members. Not all homes were filled; even morning prayer eventually became suspended. To explain the decline, some participants alluded to personality conflicts or financial constraints.

In *The Little Gidding Way* Robert Van de Weyer had noted history's "numerous experiments in community life for families," warning prophetically: "Sadly few have survived, many collapsing within a short time, mainly because they have been too tight and close-knit in their pattern of life, and too high in their ideals. . . . At the heart of the Christian life there is tension between vision and practice, ideal and reality."[13]

As it turned out, the modern lay community did not outlast the twentieth century. The place itself, however, would remain open for visitors, with the Little Gidding Trust, an English nonprofit charity, continuing to maintain the property and employ caretakers.

Surrounded by fields, vulnerable to approach from any direction, Little Gidding has always offered a retreat but never a refuge. The English civil war spilled into Ferrar's chapel. Eliot's poem emerged from World War II's blitz. Van de Weyer's community, confronting the world's disorder through work and prayer, lasted nearly as long as Ferrar's; its attempt at faithfulness did not guarantee longevity. As a visitor, I found myself beholden to it for a witness that welcomed guests, preserved the chapel, and kindled prayer life as long as it could. Eliot might have been describing its household when he wrote in another corner of *Four Quartets:*

> For us, there is only the trying. The rest is not our business.[14]

My reverie this fresh March morning is broken by a horse and rider, out for exercise from a neighboring farm. Not far away from these fields lie the towns of John Bunyan's Bedford and John Newton's Olney. "Little Gidding," *The Pilgrim's Progress,* and "Amazing Grace" all trace their roots to within a few miles of one another, making this corner of rural England unsurpassed for devotional legacies.

Yet as I walk back to the chapel, past bursts of white blossoms in blackthorn bushes, I consider what part of Britain would not disclose legacies of faith across its terrain? If we had eyes to see, would not all the world's landscapes reveal themselves sown with stories left by people marking places where for them eternity has broken in? Eliot himself admitted he could have chosen any number of locales besides Little Gidding:

> . . .There are other places
> Which also are the world's end, some at the sea jaws,
> Or over a dark lake, in a desert or a city . . . [15]

He once identified the "other places" he had in mind: "some at the sea jaws" included Iona and the Holy Island of Lindisfarne; "dark lake" meant the lake by Saint Kevin's hermitage of Glendalough in Ireland's county Wicklow; "desert" referred to the Egyptian wilderness of the desert fathers and mothers, while "city" was St. Antony's Padua in Italy.[16]

All were settings where people had steeped themselves in prayer. Biography had quickened topography, people finding in each locale a deepening sense of dependence on God. As Little Gidding and other sites testified, Christian community has always encompassed places as well as people.

━━

The chapel is nearly as cold this spring morning as I had first found it in winter. Today, however, a current of birdsong from the woodland pours through the open door. Deborah greets me as I step into the slender nave. She points out bronze tablets on the wall, engraved with the Lord's Prayer, Apostles' Creed, and Ten Commandments, the metal radiant with morning light as though lit from within.

I glance over the chapel's visitors' book for my own name from prior years, but my earlier stays predated these pages. At least a fifth of the signatures show addresses from overseas. Along with spiritual reflections and scrawled prayers, comments pay literary homage ("Eliot got it right") and touch on historical ties ("I am a great-granddaughter of Nicholas Ferrar's brother").

Not long before he died, Nicholas Ferrar advised his brother: "It is the right, good old way you are in; keep in it." Like an echo from Isaiah 30:21—"This is the way; walk in it"—Ferrar's epigraph suggests a journey deeper into God. Meant to reassure his own community on their path of prayer and work, Ferrar's words, memorialized in lead in the chapel's oratory window, seem to encourage contemporary travelers navigating their own journey.

On the wall of the chapel I read this excerpt, embroidered and framed, from "Little Gidding":

> The communication of the dead
> is tongued with fire beyond the language of the living.[17]

The chapel evokes names of past visitors in person and in poem: Nicholas Ferrar and his extended household; George Herbert and T. S. Eliot; the Celtic saints, desert fathers and mothers, and medieval mystics

summoned by Eliot's verse; members of the former experiment led by
Robert Van de Weyer; countless pilgrims who have knelt "where prayer
has been valid."

On this spring morning I realize I have defined *community* too nar-
rowly in my life. Little Gidding broadens my vision beyond any local
pews. Here in one of the smallest chapels in Christendom, I glimpse
a congregation of believers—unwieldy, acrimonious, and diverse—
united by the Holy Spirit and unbounded by time. This slender sanctuary brims with the communion of saints.

The grey dawn has given way to a powder-blue sky. Deborah and I walk
to the farmhouse to collect our overnight bags. Before packing our car
we find the caretakers to thank them for their hospitality. Tireless and
gracious, they are preparing for the arrival of new guests. They expect
several Cambridge University students by noon; other visitors, unan-
nounced, may turn down the lane as well.

"As the years passed," wrote A. L. Maycock in *Nicholas Ferrar of
Little Gidding*, "nearly every day would bring some unexpected visitor to their doors."[18] This continues to be true nearly four centuries after
Ferrar's time. Temporal communities have come and gone, and pilgrims,
attentive in the silence, rest only briefly here. "Little Gidding" remains
a poem for travelers:

> We shall not cease from exploration
> And the end of all our exploring
> Will be to arrive where we started
> And know the place for the first time.[19]

For the conclusion of "Little Gidding," Eliot borrowed a promise
of reassurance from Julian of Norwich. With her penetrating vision of
God's love for all creation, the fourteenth-century mystic insisted that
in spite of sin "all will be well, and all will be well, and every kind of
thing will be well."[20]

Her words, adopted by Eliot, remain among the most consoling
in literature. During times of disorder Deborah and I quote them to

each other as a kind of verbal talisman. Grounded not in optimism but in relationship, Julian's vision recalls Jesus' promise: "Abide in me as I abide in you" (John 15:4). Ultimately "all will be well" not because of human ascent but divine descent.

From the low Norwich marshes and Little Gidding's pastures, Julian and Eliot could see an astounding distance, their clarity glimpsing a far country of people and place in union with God. Deborah and I consider our map of Britain, marked and faded with journeys over the years—from holy islands on ragged coasts to a chapel at the center of England. The landscape has provided places to pause and take bearings in prayer. In each setting down through the centuries, men and women have listened to what the Holy Spirit might bring to remembrance.

The morning is getting on. We take off our sweaters in the warm spring air and leave Little Gidding along a lane lined with sycamore, ash, and oak. It is a fine day for travel.

Travel Notes

Even though this book is not a travel guide in the usual sense, we thought it might help readers planning to visit these places if we shared our own practical experience traveling to, and spending reflective time in, the various landscapes we have chronicled.

In earlier times of pilgrimage, the journey served as an integral part of the experience: a lengthy time, not unlike the liturgical seasons of Advent and Lent, to prepare for an encounter with Christ and his saints. In these days of more crowded lives and rapid transit that telescopes monthlong medieval journeys into hours, modern travelers all too often arrive rushed and breathless at their destinations. While a fleeting glimpse of these places may be better than none at all, we know from our own experience how richly rewarding a more contemplative approach can be.

Therefore, in addition to practical travel information (which, given the frequency of changes, should be confirmed by Internet or telephone), we have included for each site the titles of some books that have deepened our own appreciation of these people and the places associated with them. We highly recommend, if possible, reading something about the life of the person before you arrive, and timing your visit to maximize the chances of your stay having a meditative quality. The people we have written about have confirmed our own sense of the reality and privilege of living "surrounded by so great a cloud of witnesses." We have found it worthwhile to do all we could to be fully present to what God might bring to our remembrance in these places.

Although the authors have made every effort to provide the most up-to-date and accurate information possible, the authors and publisher specifically disclaim any and all liability arising directly or indirectly from the use or application of any information contained in these Travel Notes. Please be advised that travel information is subject to change at any time. We suggest that readers write or call ahead for confirmation when making travel plans.

Whithorn (Saint Ninian, c. 360–c. 432)

LOCATION: Whithorn lies deep in Scotland's southwest corner, in the region of Dumfries and Galloway.

ACCESS: To reach Whithorn, the Celtic Christian site that predates Iona by 150 years, drive south 20 miles from the town of Newton Stewart. To find Ninian's sea cave, take the A746 main road out of Whithorn, turning left at a T junction to the A747, then watch for a farm track on the right leading seaward to Kidsdale Farm and a car park. Follow the signposted footpath to the cave for a 3-mile round-trip walk.

TIMES: Ninian's cave on the coast is always accessible, as is the Isle (now joined to the mainland) located 3 miles southeast of Whithorn. In the village of Whithorn itself, the Whithorn Visitor Centre opens from Apr. 1 to Oct. 31, 7 days a week, 10:30 A.M.–5:00 P.M., giving access to the priory (on the likely site of *Candida Casa*), the museums, and the archeological dig with its 1,600 years of history.

BOOKS: For background on Saint Ninian's legacy and Celtic Christianity, see: Shirley Toulson's *Celtic Journeys: In Scotland and the North of England* (London: HarperCollins Publishers, 1995); Moses Anderson's *St. Ninian: Light of the Celtic North* (London: Faith Press, 1964); Ian Bradley's *The Celtic Way* (London: Darton Longman & Todd, 2003) and *Colonies of Heaven: Celtic Models for Today's Church* (London:

Darton Longman & Todd, 2000); Deborah Cronin's *Holy Ground: Celtic Christian Spirituality* (Nashville, Tenn.: Upper Room Books, 1999); Philip Sheldrake's *Living Between Worlds: Place and Journey in Celtic Spirituality* (London: Darton Longman & Todd, 1995); Cintra Pemberton's *Soulfaring: Celtic Pilgrimages Then and Now* (Harrisburg, Pa.: Morehouse Publishing, 1999); and Mary C. Earle and Sylvia Maddox's *Praying with the Celtic Saints: Companions for the Journey* (Winona, Minn.: Saint Mary's Press, 2000). For a detailed description of Whithorn's excavation, see Peter Hill's *Whithorn and St. Ninian: The Excavation of a Monastic Town, 1984–91* (Whithorn, Scotland: The Whithorn Trust, 1997). For Whithorn and other sites in the United Kingdom, see Martin Palmer and Nigel Palmer's helpful guide, *The Spiritual Traveler: The Guide to Sacred Sites and Pilgrim Routes in Britain* (Mahwah, N.J.: Hidden Spring, 2000).

ENVIRONS: Neighboring Wigtown, 10 miles north of Whithorn, tells a sobering account of religious conflict and courage at the site where two women Covenantors, after refusing to recognize the king's supremacy over Christ in ecclesiastical matters, drowned in 1685 while tied to stakes in a tidal estuary.

FURTHER INFORMATION: (Telephone numbers shown as when calling from the United States. Within Britain "01" replaces all numbers in parentheses.)
- Web sites: whithorn.com; galloway.co.uk
- The Whithorn Trust Visitor Centre: tel.: (011-44-1) 988-500-508; address: 45-47 George Street, Whithorn, DG8 8NS, Scotland, UK
- Dumfries & Galloway Tourist Board: tel.: (011-44-1) 387-253-862

Iona (Saint Columba, 521–97)

LOCATION: A tiny island off the west coast of the Isle of Mull, in the Hebrides, off the west coast of Scotland.

ACCESS: Iona is accessible only by ferry, and all the ferry service in these parts is controlled by Caledonian MacBrayne. In the late 1930s when the fledgling Iona Community was working to rebuild the abbey—and finding the ferries uncooperative about supplying and landing the materials required—the workers sang the following as they worked:

> The Earth belongs unto the Lord
> And all that it contains
> Except West Highland ports and piers,
> For they are all MacBrayne's.

From Oban on the west coast, a bus usually meets the car ferry at Craignure and transports passengers across Mull to Fionnphort, where a smaller (passenger only) ferry will take you the final five minutes across to Iona. Coordinating all this with bus or train schedules to Oban is tricky, but waiting is part of the journey. Take a book, and allow a full day to travel between Edinburgh or Glasgow and Iona. You can drive and take car ferries as far as the end of Mull, but no visitors are allowed to take cars onto Iona. You can "do" Iona as a day trip, but a longer visit, if you can manage it, will be amply rewarded.

TIMES: From November to April, most things in the Islands slow down, and ferry services are cut back—sometimes by a curtailed winter schedule, sometimes by storms. The abbey is open, though, almost all year, and regular worship services are held. On Tuesdays, someone from the abbey leads a half-day pilgrimage walk around the island that is well worth doing.

BOOKS: Ronald Ferguson's *George MacLeod: Founder of the Iona Community* (London: HarperCollins, 1990) is excellent for the recent part of the abbey's history; an attractive illustrated book is E. Mairi

MacArthur's *Iona,* 2d ed. (Edinburgh: Edinburgh University Press, 2002); a nice pocket-size guide by the warden of the Iona Abbey, Peter W. Millar, is *Iona: Pilgrim's Guide* (London: Canterbury Press Norwich, 2000).

The classic biography of Saint Columba is still Adamnan's *The Life of Saint Columba,* available in a facsimile reprint (Llanerch, Wales: Llanerch Press, 1988) of the 1874 Historians of Scotland edition by Edmonston and Douglas. See also Ian Bradley's biography, *Columba: Pilgrim and Penitent* (Glasgow: Wild Goose Publications, 1996), and numerous titles on Celtic spirituality by Esther de Waal and J. Philip Newell.

FURTHER INFORMATION: (Telephone numbers shown as when calling from the United States. Within Britain "01" replaces all numbers in parentheses.)
- Web site: ionacomm@iona.org.uk
- Wardens at the Abbey: tel.: (011-44-1) 681-700-404
- Ferry service: Caledonian MacBrayne: tel.: (011-44-8) 705-650-000; Web site: www.calmac.co.uk
- Bus service on Mull from Craignure to Fionnphort: tel.: (011-44-1) 680-812-313
- Tourist Information in Oban: tel.: (011-44-1) 631-563-122

Note: You can book accommodation (at Iona's two hotels, two retreat houses, various self-catering cottages, or private homes offering bed and breakfast) via www.a1tourism.com/uk/isle-of-iona or www.ionahostel.co.uk.

The Holy Island of Lindisfarne (Saint Aidan, d. 651, and Saint Cuthbert, 634–87)

LOCATION: Lindisfarne, also known as Holy Island, rises out of the sea 3 miles off England's northeastern coast, south of the city of Berwick-upon-Tweed.

ACCESS: To cross the 3-mile causeway to Lindisfarne, travelers must take into account the tides. Tide schedules, posted at the beginning of the causeway, are also available from the Berwick-upon-Tweed Tourist Information Centre and the Heritage Centre on Holy Island.

When driving, turn off the A1 at Beal, then head east toward the coast. Buses travel daily during certain summer months but in the off-season only on Wednesday and Saturday. The nearest train service is Berwick-upon-Tweed.

Even if you have to borrow time from the rest of your itinerary, spend at least a night or two on Lindisfarne. When the crowds leave and the tide rises to cover the causeway, a sustaining quiet settles over Holy Island. Find rest in the corners of the ruined priory, walk the remote northern edge of the island, and take part in vigils at the parish church.

TIMES: While the tide determines comings and goings, most travelers will be mindful as well of the hours of admission of the English Trust's Lindisfarne Priory and the National Trust's Lindisfarne Castle (see Web sites listed under Further Information). The island's beautiful walking paths and the parish church remain accessible at all hours.

BOOKS: Introductions to Lindisfarne are provided by David Adams's *Holy Island* (London: Canterbury Press Norwich, 1997) and Sheila Mackay's *Lindisfarne Landscapes* (Edinburgh: Saint Andrew Press, 1996). Amid the cornucopia of titles dealing with Celtic Christianity, consider Andrew Jones's *Every Pilgrim's Guide to Celtic Britain and Ireland* (Liguori, Mo.: Liguori Publications, 2002, and London: Canterbury Press Norwich, 2002), Deborah K. Cronin's *Holy Ground: Celtic Christian Spirituality*

Lindisfarne

(Nashville, Tenn.: Upper Room Books, 1999), Cintra Pemberton's *Soulfaring: Celtic Pilgrimages Then and Now* (Harrisburg, Pa.: Morehouse Publishing, 1999), Ian Bradley's *Colonies of Heaven* (London: Darton Longman & Todd, 2000) and *The Celtic Way* (London: Darton Longman & Todd, 2003), and Philip Sheldrake's *Living Between Worlds: Place and Journey in Celtic Spirituality* (London: Darton Longman & Todd, 1995). For Lindisfarne and other sites in the United Kingdom, see Charles Wilkinson's excellent, but lamentably out-of-print, *Spirit of Britain: A Pilgrimage of Faith and Pride* (Ancaster, Ontario: Pilgrim Paperbacks, 1987), and Michael Counsell's *Every Pilgrim's Guide to England's Holy Places* (London: Canterbury Press Norwich, 2003).

ENVIRONS: Not far from Lindisfarne and usually visible across the sea, the Farne Islands shelter an unmatched bird sanctuary and the site of Cuthbert's hermitage. In good weather the Farne Islands can be reached by boat from the coastal village of Seahouses.

FURTHER INFORMATION: (Telephone numbers shown as when calling from the United States. Within Britain "01" replaces all numbers in parentheses.)
- Web site: lindisfarne.org.uk
- Lindisfarne Priory and Museum: tel.: (011-44-1) 289-389-200
- Lindisfarne Heritage Centre: tel.: (011-44-1) 289-389-004
- Tourist Information in Berwick-upon-Tweed: tel.: (011-44-1) 289-330-733
- Farne Islands: Call Billy Shiel in Seahouses, England: tel.: (011-44-1) 665-720-308
- The National Trust's Lindisfarne Castle: tel.: (011-44-1) 289-389-244

199

St. Margaret's Chapel (Saint Margaret, 1047–93)

LOCATION: St. Margaret's Chapel lies within the precincts of Edinburgh Castle (under the auspices of Historic Scotland), at the heart of the Scottish capital of Edinburgh. The castle looms high at the west end of the Royal Mile, which connects the castle with the Palace of Holyrood at the east end.

ACCESS: The castle is approximately a quarter of an hour's—lovely—walk from Waverly Rail Station, or accessible by taxi or city bus. St. Margaret's Chapel is a short uphill walk from the castle entrance.

TIMES: The castle is open 7 days a week, from 9:30 A.M.–5:00 P.M. (6:00 P.M. in summer), and the chapel is always open during castle hours. On Saint Margaret's feast day (Nov. 16) there are special services; otherwise the chapel is used formally only for occasional weddings and christenings (Scottish servicemen only). Quiet prayer and meditation may be inhibited by crowds of tourists.

BOOKS: The best guide to the chapel is a wee booklet by Lucy Menzies, Ronald A. Knox, and Ronald Selby Wright, *St. Margaret Queen of Scotland and Her Chapel*, ed. Charles Robertson (Edinburgh: St. Margaret's Chapel Guild, 1994). The best full-length biography of Margaret is still Lucy Menzies, *St. Margaret Queen of Scotland*, first published in 1925, reprinted in a facsimile edition by J. M. F. Books, Llanerch, Wales, 1992. Also good is Alan J. Wilson, *St. Margaret Queen of Scotland* (Edinburgh: John Donald Publishers, 1993).

ENVIRONS: The charming town of Dunfermline, long associated with Margaret and Malcolm, is located just a few miles inland on the other side of the Firth of Forth from Edinburgh, and is accessible by train (change at Inverkeithing), public buses, or car (take the B981 north after crossing the Forth Bridge). Here one can see the Dunfermline Abbey and Palace (Historic Scotland; admission to Palace), visit

Margaret's Cave (an easy walk from town centre; inquire at abbey or town hall), and in what is now Pittencrieff Park down the hill from the abbey, see the ruins of Malcolm's Tower. The original Paton painting of Margaret and Malcolm can be seen, upon request, in an upstairs chamber in the centrally located town hall.

FURTHER INFORMATION: (Telephone numbers shown as when calling from the United States. Within Britain "01" replaces all numbers in parentheses.)
- Web sites: www.dunfabbey.freeserve.co.uk/history.htm
  www.historic-scotland.gov.uk
- Historic Scotland, Edinburgh: tel.: (011-44-1) 316-688-600
- Tourist Information, Dunfermline: tel.: (011-44-1) 383-720-999

Note: The lovely little booklet on Saint Margaret and her chapel, usually available at the castle, can also be found online at www.qmssa.org/chapel.htm. For excellent photos of the chapel, see www.cin.org/churches/margchapel.html. If your name is Margaret (and you reside in Scotland), you are eligible for membership in St. Margaret's Guild, founded in 1942 under the patronage of HRH Princess Margaret. The guild supplies fresh flowers for the chapel altar throughout the year and publishes the booklet on the chapel, its proceeds used to support various charitable causes (of which the sainted queen would surely approve).

Canterbury Cathedral

LOCATION: In the city of Canterbury, county of Kent, 65 miles southeast of London.

ACCESS: Medieval pilgrims took weeks on foot or horse to reach Canterbury, a trip now possible by train in 90 minutes from London's Victoria Station to Canterbury's East Station, followed by a 10-minute walk to the cathedral.

If possible, plan to stay overnight in Canterbury, allowing time in the sanctuary in the early morning and late afternoon when the cathedral offers matins, Holy Communion, and choral evensong.

Visitors today do well to prepare before setting out, reading not only of Thomas Becket's (1118–70) life and death but also of contemporary religious persecution, given the East Chapel's dedication to the "Saints and Martyrs of Our Own Time." Other British cathedrals also illuminate such sacrifice (Westminster Abbey has filled niches over its west door with statues of twentieth-century martyrs), but Canterbury still seems to ring with the sound of swords striking stone.

TIMES: Obtain times for visiting the cathedral, as well as for worship services, via the Internet or telephone (see Further Information). Check times in advance of arrival; hours change slightly depending on the season or day of the week.

BOOKS: T. S. Eliot's *Murder in the Cathedral* (New York: Harcourt, Brace, 1963); Shirley Du Boulay's *The Road to Canterbury* (Harrisburg, Pa.: Morehouse Publishing, 1995), and former Canon Peter Brett's *Canterbury: Pilgrim's Guide* (London: Canterbury Press Norwich, 2000).

Canterbury Cathedral's East Chapel turns visitors' attention toward contemporary Christian martyrdom, a casualty toll searingly documented by Paul Marshall, *Their Blood Cries Out* (Dallas, Tex.: Word Publishing, 1997); Nina Shea, *In the Lion's Den: A Shocking Account of Persecution and Martyrdom of Christians Today and How We Should Respond* (Nashville, Tenn.: Broadman & Holman Publishers, 1997); *The International Bulletin of Missionary Research* ("Annual Statistical Table on Global Mission"); and the extraordinarily comprehensive study in David B. Barrett, Todd M. Johnson, et al., *World Christian Trends, A.D. 30–A.D. 2200: Interpreting the Annual Christian Megacensus* (Pasadena, Calif.: William Carey Library Publishers, 2001)—see part 4, "Martyrology: The Demographics of Christian Martyrdom: A.D. 33–A.D. 2001."

FURTHER INFORMATION: (Telephone numbers shown as when calling from the United States. Within Britain "01" replaces all numbers in parentheses.)
- Web site: www.canterbury-cathedral.org
- Canterbury Cathedral: tel.: (011-44-1) 227-762-862
- Canterbury Tourist Information: tel.: (011-44-1) 227-378-100

Norwich, England (Lady Julian, 1342–1413)

LOCATION: Norwich is a beautiful medieval cathedral city in the fen (marshy) country of Norfolk, within a great loop of the river Wensum. St. Julian's tiny church is tucked away in St. Julian's Alley, which runs between King Street and Rouen Road, a pleasant 10-minute walk south of the cathedral. Next to the church, to which the cell is attached, is the Julian Centre (run by the Friends of Julian of Norwich), which is an excellent source of information, maps, etc., and sells books as well. Also adjacent is All Hallows House, run by an order of Anglican sisters, where clean, quiet accommodations and simple meals are available to visitors to the shrine for a modest charge.

ACCESS: Norwich is accessible by train from Peterborough or London; the church and Julian's cell are a brief cab ride from either the train or bus station. It is a good idea to give the full address and cross-street reference to the taxi driver, as surprisingly few locals seem to know about Julian. When Deborah asked to be taken to All Hallows, the cabbie obviously thought she was going as a postulant, and wished her hearty good luck ("All the best, luv!") in her new life.

TIMES: The parish church is open during ordinary daytime hours. Check schedule for Sunday and weekday Eucharists. The sisters' own chapel at All Hallows observes daily lauds and vespers (guests are welcome to attend both services). The Julian Centre is open 11:00 A.M. to 3:00 P.M. or 4:00 P.M. (Phone first to be sure of current times.)

BOOKS: Julian's *Showings* are currently available in several editions; the Paulist Press edition, in the Classics of Western Spirituality series, has excellent notes and a good introduction. Also worthwhile is *Julian: Woman of Our Day*, ed. Robert Llewelyn (London: Darton Longman & Todd, 1985) and Robert Llewelyn's *With Pity Not with Blame: The Spirituality of Julian of Norwich and* The Cloud of Unknowing *for Today* (London: Darton Longman & Todd, 1989). See also *Encounter with*

God's Love: Selected Writings of Julian of Norwich, compiled by Keith Beasley-Topliffe (Nashville, Tenn.: Upper Room Books, 1998).

ENVIRONS: No visit to Norwich or to Julian's cell would be complete without a visit to the splendid Norwich Cathedral, which Julian no doubt frequented before entering her anchor hold, and where there is a commemorative stained-glass window honoring her. The cathedral, Norman in style, is built of honey-colored stone; construction began in 1096 and was completed in 1145, so it was already two hundred years old when Julian was born. Don't miss the fourteenth-century bronze pelican lectern in the choir. If you have the time, by all means walk from the shrine to the cathedral and back again to get a sense of some of Julian's own geography: she surely walked this route, along these streets, before she entered her cell.

FURTHER INFORMATION: (Telephone numbers shown as when calling from the United States. Within Britain "01" replaces all numbers in parentheses.)
- The Julian Centre: tel.: (011-44-1) 603-767-380; e-mail: TheJulianCentre@ukgateway.net; address: St. Julian's Alley, Rouen Road, Norwich, England NR1 1QT. The Centre is the best source of information about the church and shrine.
- All Hallows House: tel.: (011-44-1) 603-624-738; address: Rouen Road, Norwich, England NR1 1QT.
- Norwich Tourist Information: tel.: (011-44-1) 603-727-927 or the Web site www.norwich.gov.uk can help with accommodations, etc., if you choose not to stay at the All Hallows Guesthouse (although we highly recommend the sisters' hospitality).

Note: The Friends of Julian of Norwich, a registered charity, supports the work of the Julian Shrine, encourages interest in Julian's writings, and continues her work of prayer throughout the world. They also publish a newsletter twice a year and on the second Saturday in May host a Julian Festival, with a guest speaker and a picnic lunch. Further information may be obtained from the Centre at the address above.

Also, the "Julian Meetings" consist of several hundred small groups in Britain and elsewhere who, in the tradition of Lady Julian, meet regularly for the practice of contemplative prayer. JM also publish a magazine three times a year. For more information, phone (011-44-1) 527-892-372.

Bemerton Village (George Herbert, 1593–1633)

LOCATION: St. Andrew's parish church, which George Herbert served as rector (1630–33), is located in the village of Bemerton, about 1½ miles west of the cathedral town of Salisbury, in south Wiltshire, 90 miles from London in southwest England. The tiny stone church, which dates to the thirteenth century, is on the country road (not the main highway, the A30-A36 just to the north) that links Salisbury to Wilton.

ACCESS: *Beware:* Although Bemerton is between Salisbury and Wilton, the Wilton bus service from Salisbury does not go through Bemerton. You can get to Bemerton by car (or taxi from the Salisbury railway station) by following the Churchfields Road from just south of the train station through the Churchfields Industrial Estate, which is just as soulless and dispiriting as it sounds. It is also possible, although it can be slightly dangerous, to walk this way, about three-quarters of an hour on foot from the center of Salisbury. Either way, you can't miss the church: it is right on the road, on the right-hand side, at the far end of the village.

A compromise pedestrian route to and from Salisbury involves braving the fumes and proximity of the traffic by walking the sure way, along this road, but then returning along the river Nadder, cutting across the water meadows back to Salisbury.

To walk this way, with the spire of Salisbury Cathedral ever in view, is to follow in George Herbert's footsteps: this was his route, from the bottom of the old rectory garden, into town twice a week to make music with his friends in the cathedral Close. Even in dry weather, this walk can be damp but peaceful and lovely; ask the current rectory residents for permission to cross the bridge over the river at the bottom of the garden, and follow the Harnham village signs to the Town Path; you will end up (in, again, about three-quarters of an hour) just west of the cathedral in Queen Elizabeth Gardens.

The church may be locked; if so, consult the notice in the porch for instructions on obtaining the key. Access to the church is free, although donations are welcome; access to the old rectory, now privately owned, is by permission only.

TIMES: St. Andrew's Church is still used for weddings and occasional services; consult the notice board in the church porch for details. One may obtain the key at any reasonable time and stay as long as one likes. Be sure to lock up again when you leave, and remember to return the key.

ENVIRONS: It would be a pity, as well as a practical impossibility, to visit Bemerton without passing through the medieval city of Salisbury, with its early English cathedral, whose elegant spire, famous from Constable's paintings, is the tallest in England. George Herbert was ordained here.

BOOKS: The most useful edition of Herbert's poetry and prose is from the Classics of Western Spirituality series, *George Herbert: The Country Parson, The Temple,* ed. John N. Wall Jr. (New York: Paulist Press, 1981). Amy M. Charles's *A Life of George Herbert* (Ithaca, N.Y.: Cornell University Press, 1977) is excellent. Izaak Walton's *Life of George Herbert,* first published in 1670, is a classic of Christian literature; the World's Classic edition (1923) is a treasure if you can find it second-hand. A wonderful small book is T. S. Eliot's *George Herbert,* in the Writers and Their Work series (Devon, England: Northcote House Publishers, 1996). Also very good is Philip Sheldrake's *Love Took My Hand: The Spirituality of George Herbert* (Cambridge, Mass.: Cowley Publications, 2000).

FURTHER INFORMATION: (Telephone numbers shown as when calling from the United States. Within Britain "01" replaces all numbers in parentheses.)
- Salisbury Tourist Information Centre: tel.: (011-44-1) 722-334-956; Web site: www.visitsalisbury.com
- Salisbury Cathedral: tel.: (011-44-1) 722-555-120

The village of Bemerton itself boasts neither a hotel nor a pub, but accommodation and meals are available along the Town Path, on the river, and at the Old Mill Hotel in West Harnham; phone (011-44-1) 722-327-517 if you want to stay between Salisbury and Bemerton.

York (Margaret Clitherow, 1553–88, and Mary Ward, 1585–1643)

LOCATION: Within the precincts of medieval York, Margaret Clitherow's house has been converted to a shrine in her memory by the Catholic Women's League, who honor her as their patron (as does the Union of Catholic Mothers). The shrine is on the Shambles, adjacent to the Newgate Market, about 200 yards south of the Minster between Parliament Street and Colliergate. The place of her execution (unmarked) can be found to the south of the west end of the Ouse Bridge. Up the river just another 200 yards or so is the medieval Guildhall where Margaret Clitherow was tried and sentenced. All of this is within a touchingly small radius: she did not have far to go.

The Bar Convent, founded by one of Mary Ward's companion "English Ladies," is still at 17 Blossom Street, just outside the city walls at the west gate, the Micklegate Bar. The first two floors of the original convent building are now an excellent museum; upstairs is where the resident sisters still live, and where, in a different wing, overnight bed-and-breakfast accommodation is available.

ACCESS: Getting to York is fairly straightforward from any direction, by rail (about 2 hours from London Kings' Cross; about 2½ hours from Edinburgh Waverly) or by coach or by car. Don't attempt to drive a car within the city; there are park-and-ride lots outside the walls. Within the walls, nearly everything mentioned here is accessible on foot within the heart of the old city.

TIMES: The Bar Convent Museum (admission fee) and shop are open Monday to Friday; the excellent little café is open from 9:30 A.M.–5:00 P.M. Monday to Saturday. Margaret Clitherow's shrine is open "all day; every day." Mass is said every Saturday morning at 10:00 or otherwise by arrangement: Contact the parish priest at the St. Wilfrid's Catholic Church on High Petergate (Web site: www.stwilfridsyork.org.uk/st_margaret_clitherow.html). The Guildhall still houses the city of York's municipal offices and is open Monday–Friday 9:00 A.M.–5:00 P.M., Saturdays 10:00 A.M.–5:00 P.M., and Sundays 2:00–5:00 P.M.

ENVIRONS: Within the city of York, the York Minster, the largest Gothic cathedral in northern Europe, must not be missed. It is open 7:00 A.M.–5:00 P.M. in the winter, 7:00 A.M.–8:30 P.M. in the summer, and offers daily Eucharist and sung evensong.

A couple of miles past the Micklegate Bar on Blossom Street (which becomes The Mount and then Mount Vale) near the Knavesmuir Race Course, a simple stone commemorates the York Tyburn martyrs who were executed here. Margaret Clitherow used to go barefoot at night along this route to pray by the gallows. At the other end of York, just outside the eastern boundary of the city but only a couple of miles from the city center, is the village church of Osbaldwick, where Mary Ward is buried and where her gravestone can still be seen. Further afield, but worth a detour to the Yorkshire coast (about 40 miles from York), are the ruins of the abbey at Whitby, founded in 657 by Saint Hilda, host to the famous Synod of Whitby in 664 C.E. The abbey was destroyed by the Danes in 867 and refounded by the Benedictines in 1078.

BOOKS: Both Margaret Clitherow and Mary Ward have their own chapters in *Women of the Catholic Resistance in England, 1540–1680,* by Roland Connelly (Durham, England: Pentland Press, 1997), which is out of print but worth a search, and separate entries in Robert Ellsberg's *All Saints: Daily Reflections on Saints, Prophets, and Witnesses for Our Time* (New York: Crossroad Publishing Co., 1997). A biography of Mary Ward, by Henriette Peters and translated by Helen Butterworth, *Mary Ward: A World in Contemplation* (Leominster, England: Gracewing, 1994), is available at the Bar Convent bookstore. Also out of print but worth a search is *Mary Ward (1585–1646)* by Mary Oliver (New York: Sheed & Ward, 1959). The Catholic Truth Society (London) has published two fine booklets on Mary Ward available at the Bar Convent: *Mary Ward (1585–1645): A Woman for All Seasons* by Mary Margaret Littlehales, 1974; and *Mary Ward: Once and*

Future Foundress by M. Emmanuel Orchard, 1985. Also edited by M. Emmanuel Orchard is *Till God Will: Mary Ward through Her Writings* (London: Darton Longman & Todd, 1985). No full-length biography on Margaret Clitherow seems to be in print at the moment, but there is an excellent booklet by Philip Caraman, *Margaret Clitherow* (London: Catholic Truth Society, 1986). Another booklet (60 pages, paperback) is by John Rayne-Davis, *Margaret Clitherow: Saint of York* (Beverley, England: Highgate Publications Ltd., 2002).

FURTHER INFORMATION: (Telephone numbers shown as when calling from the United States. Within Britain "01" replaces all numbers in parentheses.)

- The Bar Convent: tel.: (011-44-1) 904-643-238

    Web site: www. bar-convent.org.uk

    e-mail: info@bar-convent.org.uk

- York Tourist Information: tel.: (011-44-1) 904-621-756

    Web site: www.visityork.org.uk

Note: The Bar Convent offers bed and self-serve breakfast in 15 pleasant rooms (8 singles, 6 twins, 1 double) at reasonable rates.

Pendle Hill (George Fox, 1624–91)

LOCATION: Pendle Hill rises above the villages of Barley and Downham in England's county of Lancashire, east of the town of Clitheroe, near the Yorkshire border.

ACCESS: Only walking will take you to the top of Pendle Hill, but a car is needed to reach its base. The nearest train station is in Clitheroe. Even with good local maps (as David found when he returned to climb Pendle) a driver still encounters a confusing maze of under-signed country roads on the way to Barley and Downham.

From the base of Pendle Hill, walkers can reach the summit in two hours. More than a half-dozen paths of varying grade wind to the top. Take walking clothes and suitable weather gear. For more information about Pendle Hill, see Elfrida Vipont Foulds's *The Birthplace of Quakerism: A Handbook for the 1652 Country* (London: Quaker Home Service, 1987).

TIMES: Hill walkers ascend Pendle Hill throughout the year, taking care as always for sudden changes in the weather and the possibility of hill-fog, highly disorienting even when a compass is available.

BOOKS: For a description of the years surrounding his Pendle Hill experience, see George Fox, *The Journal of George Fox* (London: Penguin Books, 1998). For insight into Fox's legacy and the evolution of Quaker faith and witness, consider: Howard Brinton, *Friends for 300 Years* (London: George Allen & Unwin, 1953), rev. ed. Margaret Hope Bacon (Wallingford, Pa.: Pendle Hill Publications, 2002); Elfrida Vipont, *The Story of Quakerism, 1652–1952* (London: Bannisdale Press, 1954); Thomas R. Kelly, *A Testament of Devotion* (New York: Harper & Row Publishers, 1941); Jessamyn West, ed., *The Quaker Reader* (Wallingford, Pa: Pendle Hill Publications, 1962); and Ronald Blythe's beautiful *Divine Landscapes: A Pilgrimage through Britain's Sacred Places* (London: Canterbury Press Norwich, 1998).

ENVIRONS: Within a few hours' drive northwest of Pendle, numerous areas are associated with the early days of Quakerism, including Settle, Sedburgh, and Firbank Fell. Further afield, Ulverston's Swarthmoor Hall operates in part as a retreat center and is open at times for visitors and by appointment.

FURTHER INFORMATION: (Telephone numbers shown as when calling from the United States. Within Britain "01" replaces all numbers in parentheses.)

- Clitheroe Tourist Information Centre: tel.: (011-44-1) 200-425-566
- Swarthmoor Hall: tel.: (011-44-1) 229-583-204
  Web site: www.swarthmoorhall.co.uk

Aldersgate Street & Wesley's Chapel and House
(John Wesley, 1703–91)

LOCATION: Aldersgate Street winds through London north of St. Paul's Church, but the site of John Wesley's conversion (most probably 28 Aldersgate Street in Nettleton Court) is gone, much of the area obliterated by World War II bombs and postwar development. That said, Wesley's story remains particularly visible at the Conversion Place Memorial and a mile away at London's City Road complex of Wesley's house, chapel, and the Museum of Methodism.

ACCESS: Begin at Aldersgate Street at the John Wesley Conversion Place Memorial, located next to the front entrance of Museum of London and accessible by bus, taxi, or the underground (Barbican and St. Paul's are the nearest tube stations). The mammoth bronze sculpture that displays a page from Wesley's *Journal* entry of Wednesday, May 24, 1738, can be reached from Aldersgate Street by ascending steps to the pedestrian walkway. For a moment of quiet, cross down the street into St. Botulph's Church and the nearby garden of Postman Park, a patch of green in a concrete sea.

From Aldersgate a 15-minute walk or short taxi ride brings you to City Road Chapel, Wesley's house and tomb, and the Museum of Methodism at 49 City Road. (Nearest tube stations are Moorgate or Old Street—Exit 4.)

TIMES: Aldersgate's open-air Conversion Place Memorial can be visited at any hour. See Web site in Further Information for hours of Wesley's house and the Museum of Methodism, as well as hours for services at City Road Chapel.

BOOKS: Follow Wesley's account of the years surrounding Aldersgate in *The Journal of John Wesley,* ed. Elisabeth Jay (New York: Oxford University Press, 1987) and *A Longing for Holiness: Selected Writings of John Wesley,* Upper Room Spiritual Classics, ed. Keith Beasley-Topliffe

(Nashville, Tenn.: Upper Room Books, 1997). From W. H. Fitchett's *Wesley and His Century: A Study in Spiritual Forces* (London: Smith, Elder, & Co., 1906) to Roy Hattersley's *A Brand from the Burning: The Life of John Wesley* (New York: Doubleday, 2003), many titles illuminate Wesley's faith and legacy. T. E. Dowley's *Through Wesley's England* (Nashville, Tenn.: Abingdon Press, 1988) offers a visual introduction to Wesley's peripatetic witness. *A Methodist Guide to London and the South-east,* compiled by John A. Vickers and Betty Young (Methodist Publishing House, 1991), is another excellent resource.

ENVIRONS: Directly across from City Road Chapel, take time to walk through Bunhill Fields, the burial ground for William Blake, John Bunyan, Daniel Defoe, Isaac Watts, Susanna Wesley (mother of John), and "a thousand dissenters."

FURTHER INFORMATION: (Telephone numbers shown as when calling from the United States. Within Britain "020" replaces all numbers in parentheses.)
- Web sites: www.wesleyschapel.org.uk; methodist.org.uk
- Wesley's Chapel: tel.: (011-44-20) 7253-2262; address: City Road Chapel, 49 City Road, London EC1Y 1AU, England.

Olney (John Newton, 1725–1807)

LOCATION: The market town where John Newton wrote "Amazing Grace" and other hymns is found in Buckinghamshire, on the river Great Ouse, about 60 miles northwest of London.

ACCESS: Olney can be reached most easily by car (from London follow the M1 to Junction 14, then to the A509). Bus service from London is possible, but the nearest train station is Milton Keynes or Bedford.

Off the beaten track of many itineraries (though not on Shrove Tuesday, see below), this town gave its name through the *Olney Hymns* to perhaps more of the world's enduring hymns than any locale. Before going, consider Newton's and Cowper's prolific contributions to hymn books, their verses born of firsthand experience with sin and God's mercy. Though Olney's mercantile bustle rarely lends itself to a contemplative retreat, set aside time in the parish church and the garden behind "Orchard Side" (now the Cowper and Newton Museum), particularly the summer house where Cowper wrote many of his hymns and poems.

TIMES: Olney's Parish Church of St. Peter and St. Paul is open during daylight hours, with morning prayer daily at 9:00 A.M. and Sunday's main service at 10:00 A.M. For opening hours of the Cowper and Newton Museum, see the Web sites listed in Further Information.

Every year on Shrove Tuesday local runners carry pancakes in frying pans to compete in a race from the Market Place to the Parish Church. The race (linked to one held in Liberal, Kansas) ends with the Annual Shriving Service in the church, during which, according to local residents, "half a dozen of Newton's and Cowper's hymns are sung with great gusto and in fine style."

BOOKS: The story of John Newton and his most famous hymn is chronicled in Steve Turner's *Amazing Grace: The Story of America's Most*

Beloved Song (New York: HarperTrade, 2002). For additional sketches of Newton's life and conversion, consider Brian H. Edwards's *Through Many Dangers: The Story of John Newton* (Welwyn, England: Eurobooks, 1975), Bernard Martin's *An Ancient Mariner: A Biography of John Newton* (London: Epworth Press, 1960), and D. Bruce Hindmarsh's *John Newton and the English Evangelical Tradition* (Grand Rapids, Mich.: William B. Eerdmans Publishing Co., 2000). Newton's own *Collected Letters* (London: Trafalgar Square Publishing, 1989) offers examples of his insightful spiritual correspondence. The museum stocks numerous titles about both Newton and Cowper, including facsimile copies of their *Olney Hymns*.

ENVIRONS: Within easy driving distance of Olney are Little Gidding, Coventry Cathedral, and Bedford, where John Bunyan wrote *The Pilgrim's Progress*.

FURTHER INFORMATION: (Telephone numbers shown as when calling from the United States. Within Britain "01" replaces all numbers in parentheses.)
- Web site: mkheritage.co.uk (see Cowper and Newton Museum)
- The Cowper and Newton Museum. tel.: (011-44-1) 234-711-516; e-mail: museum@olney.co.uk; address: Orchard Side, Market Place, Olney, Buckinghamshire, MK46 4AJ, England.
- Bedford Tourist Information: tel.: (011-44-1) 234-215-226
- Milton Keynes Tourist Information: tel.: (011-44-1) 908-358-300

St. Beuno's and St. Winefred's Well
(Gerard Manley Hopkins, 1844–89)

LOCATION: St. Beuno's Ignatian Spirituality Centre lies halfway between the tiny villages of Rhuallt and Tremeirchion just off the B5429. St. Winefred's Well is in nearby Holywell (it's best to order a taxi by phone from St. Beuno's or from Rhyl if you don't have your own car), a place of pilgrimage since the seventh century.

ACCESS: The nearest rail station (as well as the nearest National Express bus stop) is in "frail, shallow" Rhyl (as Hopkins called it), on the North Wales coastline. There are usually taxis at the station as well as in Water Street near the town hall.

The A55 Expressway now bypasses Rhuallt. If traveling east or west on the A55, look for exits signed Rhuallt B5429. In the village of Rhuallt, opposite the Smithy Arms, take the road to Tremeirchion and Bodfari. St. Beuno's is the first left turn after about half a mile.

TIMES: If you aren't able to stay for a retreat and just want to look around, be sure to phone or write ahead for permission and check in with the office on arrival. Increasingly, St. Beuno's specializes in 3-month sabbatical courses and the traditional 30-day retreat using Ignatius's *Spiritual Exercises,* but the Centre still offers short retreats.

The shrine of St. Winefred's Well in Holywell is visible from the street and open most days. There are daily services in the summer and weekly (Sunday afternoon) in the winter; phone the custodian at (011-44-1) 352-713-054 to make special arrangements.

ENVIRONS: There are marvelous walks in the vicinity of St. Beuno's, many of them full of echoes of the poetry of Hopkins. The charming village of Tremeirchion is within easy walking distance by road; don't miss the atmospheric parish church with its ancient yew trees in the churchyard.

BOOKS: *The Poems of Gerard Manley Hopkins,* 4th ed., ed. W. H. Gardner (New York: Oxford University Press, Inc., 1976) is regarded as the standard work. First published in 1953, this selection of poems and prose (including many letters) is augmented by good notes and an excellent introduction. Also available in a Penguin edition. Robert Bernard Martin's biography *Gerard Manley Hopkins: A Very Private Life* (New York: G. P. Putnams' Sons, 1991) is excellent. *Gerard Manley Hopkins: A Jesuit in Poets' Corner* by William Van Etten Casey (Chicago: Loyola University Press, 1990) consists of a biographical essay and a one-man play originally titled *Immortal Diamond.*

FURTHER INFORMATION: (Telephone numbers shown as when calling from the United States. Within Britain "01" replaces all numbers in parentheses.)
- Web site: members.aol.com/StBeunos
- St. Beuno's Ignatian Spirituality Centre: tel.: (011-44-1) 745-583-444; fax: (011-44-1) 745-584-151; e-mail: StBeunos@aol.com; address: St. Asaph, Denbighshire, North Wales LL17 OAS, UK.
- St. Winefred's Well, Custodian: tel.: (011-44-1) 352-713-054

Pleshey Retreat House (Evelyn Underhill, 1875–1941)

LOCATION: The Diocesan House of Retreat lies on the edge of the village of Pleshey, 8 miles north of Chelmsford, 40 miles from London.

ACCESS: From London (Liverpool Street Station) trains direct to Chelmsford run frequently; the journey from London takes about three-quarters of an hour. There is a weekday bus service (No. 52) from the Chelmsford Railway Station, and cabs are always available at the train station. The House publishes a full schedule of retreats and quiet days and welcomes individual as well as group bookings. There are 22 single bedrooms in the House; one on the ground floor is handicapped-accessible. A thatched cottage in the garden can sleep five. (Be warned: Pleshey is so tiny that one cannot buy so much as a newspaper, although there is a White Horse pub across from the retreat house where one can get a meal.)

TIMES: The House is closed for Christmas, Easter, and summer holidays. Services in the chapel are offered in conjunction with scheduled retreats. The House of course protects the silence of those on retreat; it would be a good idea to write or call before arriving to ask permission to look around, if unable to stay for a retreat.

BOOKS ABOUT EVELYN UNDERHILL: The classic biography is still Margaret Cropper's *Life of Evelyn Underhill* (New York: Harper, 1958), recently reissued by Skylight Paths Publishing (Woodstock, Vt.: 2003), with a foreword by Dana Greene; also excellent is Dana Greene's *Evelyn Underhill: Artist of the Infinite Life* (New York: Crossroad Publishing Co., 1990). Don't miss *The Letters of Evelyn Underhill*, ed. Charles Williams (London: Longmans, Green & Co., 1943) or *Collected Papers of Evelyn Underhill*, ed. Lucy Menzies (London: Longmans, Green & Co., 1946). Good anthologies include *An Anthology of the Love of God, from the Writings of Evelyn Underhill*, ed. Lumsden Barkway and Lucy Menzies (New York: D. McKay Co.,

1954), *Lent with Evelyn Underhill,* 2d ed., ed. G. P. Mellick Belshaw (Harrisburg, Pa.: Morehouse Publishing, 1990), and *Evelyn Underhill: Essential Writings,* Modern Spiritual Masters Series, ed. Emilie Griffin (Maryknoll, N.Y.: Orbis Books, 2003). Disturbing, poignant, and full of insight is *Fragments from an Inner Life: The Notebooks of Evelyn Underhill,* ed. Dana Greene (Harrisburg, Pa.: Morehouse Publishing, 1993).

BOOKS BY EVELYN UNDERHILL (based on her Pleshey retreat addresses): *Concerning the Inner Life* (New York: E. P. Dutton & Company, 1926); *The House of the Soul: Concerning the Inner Life* (Minneapolis, Minn.: Seabury Press, 1984); *The Golden Sequence: A Fourfold Study of the Spiritual Life* (London: Metheun & Co., 1932); *The Mount of Purification, with Meditations and Prayers* (London: Longmans, 1960); *Light of Christ* (Harrisburg, Pa.: Morehouse Publishing, 1989)—limited availability; *The School of Charity: Meditations on the Christian Creed* (New York: Longmans, Green and Co., 1934); *Abba: Meditations Based on the Lord's Prayer* (New York: Longmans, Green, 1940); *The Mystery of Sacrifice: A Meditation in the Liturgy* (Harrisburg, Pa.: Morehouse Publishing, 1991); and *The Fruits of the Spirit* (Harrisburg, Pa.: Morehouse Publishing, 1982). See also *The Ways of the Spirit,* 2d ed., ed. Grace Adolphsen Brame (New York: Crossroad Publishing Co., 1993) and *The Soul's Delight: Selected Writings of Evelyn Underhill,* compiled by Keith Beasley-Topliffe (Nashville, Tenn.: Upper Room Books, 1998).

FURTHER INFORMATION: (Telephone numbers shown as when calling from the United States. Within Britain "01" replaces all numbers in parentheses.)
- Pleshey's Diocesan House of Retreat: tel.: (011-44-1) 245-237-251 (if possible, call between 9:30 A.M.–12:30 P.M. Monday–Friday); fax: (011-44-1) 245-237-594; Web site: www.retreathousepleshey.com; e-mail: info@retreathouse-pleshey.com.
- Address: Pleshey, Chelmsford, Essex CM3 1HA, England

Coventry Cathedral

LOCATION: Coventry Cathedral, with new and old cathedral side by side, anchors the city of Coventry, 100 miles northwest of London, in the county of Warwickshire.

ACCESS: Coventry can easily be reached from London by rail (90 minutes from Euston Station). If possible, take part in choral evensong, when worshipers, invited to sit in the chancel if there's room, look down the nave into the bombed-out ruins. The cathedral's architecture and history have deepened many visitors' understanding of forgiveness.

TIMES: Opening hours and times of services can vary somewhat throughout the year *(call ahead or see times listed on the Internet)*. Coventry's Litany of Reconciliation is said every Friday at noon in the ruins of the old cathedral.

BOOKS: Though books about Coventry are not easy to find, for a sense of the cathedral's rebuilding, look for: Basil Spence's *Phoenix at Coventry: The Building of a Cathedral* (London: Geoffrey Bles, 1962), *Coventry Cathedral: After the Flames* and *Coventry Cathedral* (n.p.: Jarrold Colour Publications, n.d.), and John Thomas's *Coventry Cathedral* (New York: HarperCollins Publishers, 1987)—limited availability.

FURTHER INFORMATION: (Telephone numbers shown as when calling from the United States. Within Britain "024" replaces all numbers in parentheses.)
- Web site: www.coventrycathedral.org
- Coventry Cathedral: tel.: (011-44-24) 7652-1200
- Coventry Tourist Information: tel.: (011-44-24) 7622-7266
- The Community of the Cross of Nails (U.S. office): St. James Church, P.O. Box 4463, Jackson, MS 39296

Oxford (C. S. Lewis, 1898–1963)

LOCATION: Oxford is about 50 miles northwest of London, easily reached by train, bus, or car from anywhere in England. Magdalen College (founded in 1458, pronounced "maudlin") is at the far east edge of the city, on the north side of High Street between Longwall Street and the river Cherwell, opposite the Botanic Gardens. The rooms that Lewis occupied for twenty-nine years are in the "New" Building (built in the eighteenth century), overlooking the deer park to the north and Magdalen Tower to the south.

The Kilns, Lewis's home for so many years, is at Headington Quarry (now part of Risinghurst), a 20-minute bus ride (take the Cityline bus no. 22 from the train station or the Queen Street bus stop) along the London Road to the east of Oxford, via Headington, to Risinghurst. The Kilns is approached via Lewis Close; Holy Trinity Church is a short walk from the house.

ACCESS: The public is admitted to the quadrangles and gardens of the university's many colleges strictly at the pleasure of the porter at the gate! By all means, try the door. By writing ahead to the Chief Bursar and securing permission in advance, Joan Myers, the photographer whose work illustrates these chapters, had no trouble gaining access to Magdalen and even penetrated the sacred precincts of Addison's Walk.

Official guided walking tours of the historic city center and some of the colleges leave the Tourist Information Centre and Carfax Tower throughout the day year-round.

The Kilns, now owned by the C. S. Lewis Foundation, is a private residence at the moment: admission is by permission only. (Phone 909-793-0949 in the United States to reserve a tour appointment; 01-865-741-865 in the UK.)

If Holy Trinity Church is locked, the key is available at the rectory.

ENVIRONS: The whole city of Oxford is full of the presence of Lewis and his friends. Don't miss the chance to lift a memorial half-pint to the Inklings at their favorite pub, the Eagle and Child (affectionately known as the Bird and Baby), on St. Giles Street.

BOOKS BY LEWIS: Most of Lewis's own (prodigious) output is still in print; the best (subjectively speaking) are the seven *Chronicles of Narnia; Till We Have Faces: A Myth Retold; Surprised by Joy: The Shape of My Early Life; A Grief Observed; The Screwtape Letters; The Great Divorce; Mere Christianity; Letters to Malcolm: Chiefly on Prayer;* and the Perelandra trilogy.

BOOKS ABOUT LEWIS: Among Lewis's biographies, Humphrey Carpenter's *The Inklings: C. S. Lewis, J. R. R. Tolkien, Charles Williams, and Their Friends* (Boston: Houghton Mifflin and Co., 1979) is excellent; so is George Sayer's *Jack: C. S. Lewis and His Times* (San Francisco: Harper & Row, Publishers, 1988). Lewis's brother "Warnie"—W. H. Lewis—edited and wrote a poignant memoir for the *Letters of C. S. Lewis* (New York: Harcourt, Brace & World, 1966). A book that thoughtfully reveals much about the relationship between the brothers is *Brothers and Friends: The Diaries of Major Warren Hamilton Lewis,* ed. Clyde S. Kilby and Marjorie Lamp Mead (New York: Ballantine Books, 1988)—limited availability.

FURTHER INFORMATION: (Telephone numbers shown as when calling from the United States. Within Britain "01" replaces all numbers in parentheses.)
- Oxford Information Centre: tel.: (011-44-1) 865-726-871; Web site: www.visitoxford.org; address: 15–16 Broad Street, Oxford OX1 3AS, UK. The information centre provides, upon request, a special sheet of information on C. S. Lewis and is helpful with maps, directions, and information on local events and accommodations.
- Magdalen College: tel.: (011-44-1) 865-276-000
- Oxford's Cityline bus company (for service to Risinghurst and Headington): tel.: (011-44-1) 865-785-410

Note: To see photos of Magdalen College, Addison's Walk, and the Eagle and Child pub, see http://users.ox.ac.uk/~tolksoc/TolkiensOxford.

Little Gidding (Nicholas Ferrar, 1592–1637, and T. S. Eliot, 1888–1965)

LOCATION: The chapel and farm buildings that comprise Little Gidding are located about 75 miles north of London, in Cambridgeshire, near Sawtry.

ACCESS: Not an easy place to find, as most maps overlook Little Gidding. If you come from the A1 between Peterborough and Huntingdon, turn west at Sawtry, then follow the road through Glatton to the small village of Great Gidding. Turn left at the pub, then follow the road for a bit over a mile until "Little Gidding" signpost. Turn right down the long lane to reach the chapel and the farmhouse.

For an overnight stay, contact the Wardens of Little Gidding. Few places in Britain offer more reasonably priced retreat accommodations.

Little Gidding has lent its name to a chapel, a poem, and two Christian communities, and while your stay may coincide with a brief influx of day groups, more likely you will find this place "where prayer has been valid" nearly deserted and steeped in silence.

TIMES: The chapel is open until dusk every day. Visitors are welcome to stay at the farmhouse (Ferrar House) year-round.

BOOKS: Needless to say, begin with T. S. Eliot's "Little Gidding" in *Four Quartets* (New York: Harcourt, Brace and Co., 1943). Lyndall Gordon with verve and insight offers a superb biography in *T. S. Eliot: An Imperfect Life* (New York: W. W. Norton & Co., 2000). Helen Gardner illuminates in fascinating detail the evolution of "Little Gidding" in *The Composition of Four Quartets* (London: Faber and Faber, 1978).

See also Robert Van de Weyer's *Little Gidding: Story and Guide* (London: Lamp Press, 1989) and *The Little Gidding Way: Christian Community for Ordinary People* (London: Darton Longman & Todd, 1988). The Friends of Little Gidding offer a brief introduction in *Little Gidding: An Illustrated Guide* (London: Strathmore Publishing, 1998).

ENVIRONS: Follow narrow roads to nearby Olney, where John Newton and William Cowper coauthored the *Olney Hymns,* and to Bedford, where John Bunyan wrote *The Pilgrim's Progress.*

FURTHER INFORMATION: (Telephone numbers shown as when calling from the United States. Within Britain "01" replaces all numbers in parentheses.)

- Wardens at Little Gidding: tel.: (011-44-1) 832-293-383; address: Ferrar House, Little Gidding, Huntingdon, Cambridgeshire PE17 5RJ, England
- Web sites: www.littlegiddingchurch.org.uk
            www.the giddings.org.uk
- Peterborough Tourist Information: tel.: (011-44-1) 733-452-336
- Oundle Tourist Information: tel.: (011-44-1) 832-274-333

Endnotes

INTRODUCTION

1. Fiona Macleod (pen name of William Sharp) in *An Iona Anthology,* ed. F. Marian McNeill (Iona: The New Iona Press, 1990), 14.

2. John Wesley, *Journal,* 24 May 1738. See also *The Works of John Wesley* (Grand Rapids, Mich.: Zondervan Publishing House, n.d.), 1:103.

3. T. S. Eliot, "Little Gidding," in *The Complete Poems and Plays 1909–1950* (New York: Harcourt Brace Jovanovich, Publishers, 1980), 139.

4. Elizabeth Barrett Browning, "Aurora Leigh," in *The Poetical Works of Elizabeth Barrett Browning* (Boston: Houghton Mifflin, 1974), 372.

5. Gerard Manley Hopkins, *Poems and Prose of Gerard Manley Hopkins* (London: Penguin Books, 1963), 27.

6. *Collected Papers of Evelyn Underhill,* ed. Lucy Menzies (New York: Longmans, Green and Co., 1946), 196.

7. William Cowper, *Olney Hymns, In Three Books* (Olney, England: The Trustees of The Cowper and Newton Museum, 1979), Book II, Hymn 44, 234.

8. Grace Adolphsen Brame, ed. *Evelyn Underhill: The Ways of the Spirit* (New York: Crossroad Publishing Co., 1990), 15.

9. Ian Bradley, *The Celtic Way* (London: Darton Longman & Todd, 1993), 82.

CHAPTER 1: WHITHORN AND SAINT NINIAN

1. Lucy Menzies, *St. Columba of Iona* (Edinburgh: Church of Scotland Committee on Publications, 1935), 9.

2. Ian Bradley, *Colonies of Heaven* (London: Darton Longman & Todd, 2000), 204.

3. Aelred of Rievaulx, "Life of Ninian," in *Ancient Lives of Scottish Saints,* trans. W. M. Metcalfe (Paisley, Scotland: Alexander Gardner, 1895).

4. Robin Lane Fox, *Pagans and Christians* (New York: Alfred A. Knopf, 1987), 21.

5. W. Douglas Simpson, *Saint Ninian and the Origins of the Christian Church in Scotland* (Edinburgh: Oliver and Boyd, 1940), 77.

6. Ibid., 72.

7. Shirley Toulson, *Celtic Journeys* (London: Fount, 1995), 9.

8. Moses Anderson, *St. Ninian: Light of the Celtic North* (London: The Faith Press, 1964), 5.

9. Brian Blake, *The Solway Firth* (London: Robert Hale & Co., 1955), 71, quoted in Ibid., 62.

10. Lucy Menzies, *Mirrors of the Holy: Ten Studies in Sanctity* (London: A. R. Mowbray & Co., 1928), xi.

11. *Ancient Lives of Scottish Saints,* trans. W. M. Metcalfe, 19.

12. Thomas à Kempis, *The Imitation of Christ,* trans. Richard Whitford and ed. Harold C. Gardiner (Garden City, N.Y.: Image Books, 1955), 200.

CHAPTER 2: IONA AND SAINT COLUMBA

1. Ian Bradley, *Columba: Pilgrim and Penitent 597–1997* (Glasgow, Scotland: Wild Goose Publications, 1996), 25.

2. See Douglas Burton-Christie, "Into the Labyrinth: Walking the Way of Wisdom," *Weavings* 12, no. 4 (July/August 1997): 20.

3. T. S. Eliot, "Burnt Norton," in *Four Quartets* (San Diego, Calif.: Harcourt Brace & Co., 1971), 15–16.

4. John L. Paterson, *Iona: A Celebration* (London: John Murray, 1987), 10.

5. Paraphrase of the Anima Christi by David L. Fleming, in *Hearts on Fire: Praying with Jesuits,* ed. Michael Harter (St. Louis, Mo.: The Institute of Jesuit Sources, 1993), 7.

6. E. Mairi MacArthur, *Columba's Island: Iona from Past to Present* (Edinburgh: Edinburgh University Press, 1995), 45.

7. See Ronald Ferguson, *George MacLeod: Founder of the Iona Community* (London: HarperCollins, 1990).

8. MacArthur, *Columba's Island,* 45.

9. Thomas Merton, *The Seven Storey Mountain* (Garden City, N.Y.: Image Books, 1970), 508.

CHAPTER 3: THE HOLY ISLAND OF LINDISFARNE AND SAINTS AIDAN & CUTHBERT

1. David Adam, *Flame in My Heart: St. Aidan for Today* (London: Triangle, 1997), 152.

2. Bede, *Ecclesiastical History of the English People with Bede's Letter to Egbert and Cuthbert's Letter on the Death of Bede,* rev. ed., trans. Leo Sherley-Price and D. H. Farmer (London: Penguin Books, 1990),147.

3. Ibid., 170.

4. Ibid., 146.

5. Ibid., 150.

6. Ibid., 260.

7. Ibid., 257.

8. Belden C. Lane, "Landscape and Spirituality: A Tension between Place and Placelessness in Christian Thought," *The Way* Supplement 73 (Spring 1992): 5.

9. Richard Perry, *A Naturalist on Lindisfarne* (London: Lindsay Drummond, 1946), 68.

10. "A Collect for Aid Against Perils," in *The Book of Common Prayer* (New York: Oxford University Press, 1944), 31.

11. George E. Ganss., trans., *The Spiritual Exercises of Saint Ignatius* (St. Louis, Mo.: Institute of Jesuit Sources, 1992), 42.

CHAPTER 4: ST. MARGARET'S CHAPEL AND SAINT MARGARET

1. Alan J. Wilson, *St. Margaret Queen of Scotland* (Edinburgh, Scotland: John Donald Publishers, 1993), 120.

2. *Saint Margaret* [Turgot's *Life of Saint Margaret*], ed. Iain Macdonald (Edinburgh: Floris Books, 1993), 25.

3. Wilson, *St. Margaret,* 124, quoting Gordon Donaldson, *Who's Who in Scottish History,* ed. Gordon Donaldson and Robert S. Morpeth (New York: Barnes and Noble, 1973).

4. Wilson, *St. Margaret,* 124–25, quoting Gordon Donaldson, *A Northern Commonwealth: Scotland and Norway* (Edinburgh, Scotland: Saltire Society, 1993).

5. Ronald A. Knox, "A Wives' Saint," in Lucy Menzies, Ronald A. Knox, and Ronald Selby Wright, *St. Margaret Queen of Scotland and Her Chapel* (Kirkcaldy, Scotland: St. Margaret's Chapel Guild, 1957), 21.

6. Turgot does not name the venue for the Council, but see Lucy Menzies, *St. Margaret Queen of Scotland* (Llanerch, Wales: J. M. F. Books, 1992), 103.

7. Wilson, *St. Margaret,* 75.

8. See Bede, *Ecclesiastical History,* 187–92.

9. Menzies, *St. Margaret,* 103.

10. In a poignant salute to the Culdee practice of retreating to lonely places, often caves by the sea, for prayer and meditation, Margaret when in residence at Dunfermline used to retire for solitude and prayer to a cave by the Tower Burn, down the hill from Dunfermline Abbey. Once a remote spot on a wooded hillside above the stream, Margaret's cave fell into decay and was almost completely overrun by the growing town and the encroaching

motorway. The cave can still be seen, however, although access to it is across a car park and down through a long corrugated steel tunnel.

11. Menzies, *St. Margaret,* 139.

12. Sir Joseph Noel Paton painted this portrait in 1887; it is now exhibited in Dunfermline's town hall.

13. Interestingly, this very book, lost for centuries, is now in the Bodleian Library in Oxford. It was discovered in 1887 in a little parish library in Suffolk and offered for sale at Sotheby's. The Bodleian Library bought it for six pounds, and upon examining what at first appeared to be a fourteenth-century work, realized it did in fact date from the eleventh century. Moreover, some Latin verses written on the flyleaf correspond exactly with Turgot's account of the book's miraculous nonwetting. "Seeing that the Latin verses bear out Turgot's story in every detail, the book being undamaged except for two leaves at each end, which have the appearance of having been shrunk by water, experts have no hesitation in declaring this the Gospel Book of Queen Margaret" (Menzies, *St. Margaret,* 145). A facsimile of the book is now glazed and framed on the north wall of St. Margaret's Chapel, open to an illuminated page from Luke's Gospel.

14. Menzies, *St. Margaret,* 167.

15. Ibid., 173 (quoting the priest who was with Margaret at her death, as recorded by Turgot).

16. Menzies, *St. Margaret,* 176.

17. See Richard Fawcett, *The Abbey and Palace of Dunfermline* (n.p.: Historic Scotland, 1990), 16–17, for an imaginative reconstruction of the reliquary chapel.

CHAPTER 5: CANTERBURY CATHEDRAL AND THOMAS BECKET

1. Shirley Du Boulay, *The Road to Canterbury* (Harrisburg, Pa.: Morehouse Publishing, 1994), 168.

2. A. M. Allchin, telephone conversations with author, 14 November 2002; 17 November 1999.

3. Peter Brett, *Canterbury* (London: Canterbury Press Norwich, 1997) and letters to author, 3 October 2000 and 2 September 1994.

4. Nina Shea, *In the Lion's Den* (Nashville, Tenn.: Broadman & Holman Publishers, 1997), 1–2.

5. Michael Horowitz, introduction to *Their Blood Cries Out: The Worldwide Tragedy of Modern Christians Who Are Dying for Their Faith* by Paul Marshall and Lela Gilbert (Dallas, Tex.: Word Publishing, 1997), xxi.

6. David Barrett, telephone conversations with author, 11 January 2000; 18 November 2002.

7. See David B. Barrett and Todd M. Johnson, *World Christian Trends A.D. 30–A.D. 2200: Interpreting the Annual Christian Megacensus* (Pasadena, Calif.: William Carey Library Publishers), 227, 229. See also "Annual Statistical Table on Global Mission," *International Bulletin of Missionary Research,* David B. Barrett and Todd M. Johnson, and Susan Bergman, ed., *Martyrs: Contemporary Writers on Modern Lives of Faith* (Maryknoll, N.Y.: Orbis Books, 1996), 15, quoting Barrett and Johnson's *Our World and How to Reach It.* "No century has mounted so vast or sustained an attack on Christianity as the present one [the twentieth century]," says Dana Gioia, "To Witness Truth Uncompromised," in *Martyrs,* ed. Susan Bergman, 326. See also Chuck Colson, foreword to *In the Lion's Den* by Nina Shea (Nashville, Tenn.: Broadman & Holman Publishers, 1997), ix.

8. E. Martin Browne, *The Making of T. S. Eliot's Plays* (Cambridge: Cambridge University Press, 1969), 36.

9. Michael St. John Parker, ed., *Christian Canterbury: City of Pilgrims* (n.p.: Dean and Chapter of Canterbury and Pitkin Pictorials, n.d.), 8.

10. David Barrett, telephone conversations with author, 18 November 2002; 11 January 2000.

11. Geoffrey Chaucer, *The Canterbury Tales: The First Fragment,* ed. Michael Alexander (London: Penguin Books, 1996), 3.

12. Peter Brett, *Canterbury* (London: Canterbury Press Norwich, 1997), 14.

13. *John Donne: Selections from Divine Poems, Sermons, Devotions, and Prayers,* ed. John Booty (New York: Paulist Press, 1990), 272.

CHAPTER 6: NORWICH AND LADY JULIAN

1. Michael McLean, introduction to *Julian: Woman of Our Day,* ed. Robert Llewelyn (London: Darton Longman & Todd, 1985), 2.

2. *Julian of Norwich: Showings,* The Classics of Western Spirituality, trans. Edmund Colledge and James Walsh (New York: Paulist Press, 1978), 195.

3. Ibid., 186.

4. Ibid., 205.

5. Ibid., 133.

6. Ibid., 197.

7. Ibid., 342.

8. Margery Kempe (c. 1373–c. 1440) was a religious mystic whose reference to visiting Julian, in her *Book of Margery Kempe,* is the most important independent witness to Julian's historicity. See introduction to *Showings,* 18–19.

9. T. S. Eliot, "Little Gidding," in *Four Quartets* (San Diego, Calif.: Harcourt Brace & Co., 1971), 50–51.

10. *Showings,* 246.

11. This translation is from *Juliana of Norwich: Revelations of Divine Love,* trans. M. L. del Mastro (Garden City, N.Y.: Image Books, 1977), 124–25.

12. *Julian of Norwich: Showings,* 259.

13. *In Love Enclosed: More Daily Readings with Julian of Norwich,* trans. Sheila Upjohn and ed. Robert Llewelyn (London: Darton Longman & Todd, 1985), 53, 56.

14. *Julian of Norwich: Showings,* 266.

15. Ibid., 234.

16. Ibid., 201.

17. Ibid., 202.

18. Ibid., 338.

19. Ibid., 245.

20. Ibid., 238.

21. Ibid., 271.

22. Ibid., 295.

23. Ibid., 292.

24. Ibid., 301.

25. Ibid., 298.

26. Ibid., 199.

CHAPTER 7: BEMERTON AND GEORGE HERBERT

1. "When at his induction he was shut into Bemerton Church, being left there alone to toll the bell,—as the law requires him,—he stayed so much longer than an ordinary time, before he returned to those friends that stayed expecting him at the church door, that his friend Mr. Woodnot looked in at the church window, and saw him lie prostrate on the ground before the altar; at which time and place—as he after told Mr. Woodnot—he set some rules to himself, for the future manage of his life; and then and there made a vow, to labour to keep them." From Izaak Walton, *The Lives of Doctor John Donne, Sir Henry Wotton, Mr. Richard Hooker, Mr. George Herbert, and Doctor Robert Sanderson* (London: Methuen & Co., 1895), 202. Hereinafter: Walton, *The Lives.*

2. Preface to George Herbert's *The Temple* by Nicholas Ferrar (1592–1637), Anglican deacon and spiritual leader of the religious community at Little Gidding, in Huntingdonshire, England. A friend of Herbert, Ferrar served as his first literary executor. See John N. Wall Jr., ed., *George Herbert:*

The Country Parson, The Temple, Classics of Western Spirituality (New York: Paulist Press, 1981), 119.

3. Herbert, "The Temper (I)," in Wall, ed., *George Herbert,* 170.

4. Walton, *The Lives,* 191.

5. Ibid., 192.

6. John N. Wall Jr., introduction to *George Herbert,* 23.

7. Walton, *The Lives,* 192.

8. Nicholas Ferrar, preface to *The Temple* in Wall, ed., *George Herbert,* 119.

9. T. S. Eliot, *George Herbert* (Plymouth, England: Northcote House Publishers, 1994), 20.

10. Two of Herbert's older brothers, both young men of great promise, died in 1617.

11. Wall, ed., *George Herbert,* 161.

12. Ibid., 162.

13. Ibid., 290.

14. Walton, *The Lives,* 223.

15. "Submission," in Wall, ed., *George Herbert,* 214.

16. "The Church Militant," in Ibid., 317.

17. Dante Alighieri, *The Divine Comedy,* trans. John Ciardi (New York: W.W. Norton & Co., 1977), 410.

18. Colossians 3:3, in Ibid., 203.

19. Ibid., 291–92.

20. Ronald Blythe, *Divine Landscapes* (San Diego, Calif.: Harcourt Brace Jovanovich, Publishers, 1986), 132.

21. "The Windows," in Wall, ed., *George Herbert,* 183.

22. Ibid., 97.

23. "Prayer (I)," in Ibid., 166.

CHAPTER 8: YORK AND MARGARET CLITHEROW & MARY WARD

1. For a fascinating glimpse into the amazing adventures of the Jesuits in England, see Philip Caraman, *A Study in Friendship: Saint Robert Southwell and Henry Garnet* (St. Louis, Mo.: Institute of Jesuit Sources, 1991).

2. Mary Ward wished the Institute to be called Society of Jesus, like the Jesuits, which proved impossible. Her companions were long known as The English Ladies. From the middle of the eighteenth century, Mary Ward's foundation was known as the Institute of Saint Mary, which was finally granted the Ignatian Constitutions in 1978.

3. M. Gregory Kirkus, "Mary Ward" (lecture given at the Bar Convent, York, England, January 1996).

4. Margaret Mary Littlehales, *Mary Ward (1585–1645): A Woman for All Seasons* (London: Catholic Truth Society, 1974), 14.

5. *Till God Will: Mary Ward through Her Writings,* ed. M. Emmanuel Orchard (London: Darton Longman & Todd, 1985), 102.

6. Littlehales, *Mary Ward,* 31.

7. Letter from prison, 1631, quoted in M. Immolata Wetter, *Mary Ward,* trans. M. Bernadette Ganne (Regensburg, Germany: Verlag Schnell & Steiner, 1996), 18.

8. It was not until 1778 that the first Catholic Relief Act was passed by Parliament, and not until 1828 that English Catholics were allowed to vote in elections or hold public office. See David L. Edwards, *A Concise History of English Christianity from Roman Britain to the Present Day* (London: Harper Collins, 1998), 100, 107.

9. See Robert Ellsberg, *All Saints: Daily Reflections on Saints, Prophets, and Witnesses for Our Time* (New York: Crossroad Publishing Co., 1997), 41–43, 133–34.

10. Edwards, *A Concise History of English Christianity,* 54.

11. Author's paraphrase of Psalm 84:4, Book of Common Prayer.

12. John Clitherow remained Protestant all his life but loyally paid the fines for Margaret's recusancy. When she died, he wept aloud, grieving the loss of "the best wife in all England, and the best Catholic." See Philip Caraman, *Margaret Clitherow* (London: Catholic Truth Society, 1986), 14.

13. Roland Connelly, *Women of the Catholic Resistance in England, 1540–1680* (Durham, England: Pentland Press, 1997), 49.

14. Ibid., 3.

15. Ibid., 2.

16. Bossy, *The English Catholic Community,* 153, quoted in Ibid., 2.

17. Littlehales, *Mary Ward,* 4.

18. See Connelly, "Anne Clitherow," in *Women of the Catholic Resistance in England, 1540–1680,* 153–55.

CHAPTER 9: PENDLE HILL AND GEORGE FOX

1. George Fox, *The Journal,* ed. Nigel Smith (London: Penguin Books, 1998), 83; also Rufus M. Jones, ed., *The Journal of George Fox* (Richmond, Ind.: Friends United Press, 1976), 150.

2. Jones, ed., *The Journal of George Fox,* 150.

3. Ibid., 80, 82.

4. William C. Braithwaite, *The Beginnings of Quakerism,* 2d ed. (Cambridge: Cambridge University Press, 1955), 35.

5. Elfrida Vipont, *The Story of Quakerism 1652–1952* (London: Bannisdale Press, 1954), 28.

6. Jones, ed., *The Journal of George Fox,* 87.

7. From "The Holy Grail"; see Rufus M. Jones, introduction to *The Beginnings of Quakerism,* by Breathwaite, xliii.

8. Thomas R. Kelly, "The Gathered Meeting," in *The Friend* (12 December 1940): 205, quoted in Douglas V. Steere, biographical memoir, in Thomas R. Kelly, *A Testament of Devotion* (New York: Harper & Row Publishers, 1941), 24–25.

9. From a 1656 letter by George Fox written from the Launceston prison in Cornwall, in *Quaker Faith and Practice* 19 (n.p.: Yearly Meeting of the Religious Society of Friends [Quakers] in Britain, 1995): 32.

10. Jessamyn West, ed., *The Quaker Reader* (Wallingford, Pa: Pendle Hill Publications, 1962), 40.

11. Ronald Blythe, *Divine Landscapes: A Pilgrimage through Britain's Sacred Places* (London: Canterbury Press Norwich, 1998), 183.

12. Ibid., 185–86.

13. William Penn, preface to *The Journal of George Fox*, rev. ed., ed. John L. Nickalls (Cambridge: Cambridge University Press, 1952), xli.

14. Howard Brinton, *Friends for 300 Years: Beliefs and Practice of the Society of Friends Since George Fox Started the Quaker Movement* (London: George Allen & Unwin, 1953), xiii.

15. Kelly, *A Testament of Devotion,* 31.

16. D. Elton Trueblood, "Present Secular Philosophies," in *The Quaker Approach to Contemporary Problems,* ed. John Kavanaugh (London: George Allen & Unwin, 1953), 209.

CHAPTER 10: ALDERSGATE STREET AND JOHN WESLEY

1. T. S. Eliot, "Little Gidding," in *Four Quartets* (New York: Harcourt Brace Jovanovich, 1971), 51.

2. *The Works of John Wesley,* vol. 18, *Journal and Diaries (1735–8),* ed. W. Reginald Ward and Richard P. Heitzenrater (Nashville, Tenn.: Abingdon Press, 1988), 211.

3. Ibid., 249.

4. Ibid., 146.

5. George Herbert, "Love (III)," in John N. Wall Jr., ed., *George Herbert: The Country Parson, The Temple,* Classics of Western Spirituality (New York:

Paulist Press, 1981), 316.

6. *The Works of John Wesley*, ed. Ward and Heitzenrater, 249–50.

7. W. H. Fitchett, *Wesley and His Century: A Study in Spiritual Forces* (London: Smith, Elder, & Co.,1906), 281.

8. Frank Baker, *John Wesley and the Church of England* (London: Epworth Press, 1970), 54.

9. Ronald Knox, quoted in V. H. H. Green, *John Wesley* (London: Thomas Nelson and Sons, 1964), 61.

10. *The Journal of Charles Wesley*, vol. 1 (Kansas City, Mo.: Beacon Hill Press, 1980), 95.

11. T. E. Dowley, *Through Wesley's England* (Nashville, Tenn.: Abingdon Press, 1988), 88.

12. See Henry D. Rack, *Reasonable Enthusiast: John Wesley and the Rise of Methodism* (London: Epworth Press, 1992), 238.

13. *The Journal of Charles Wesley*, vol. 1, 92.

14. Charles Wesley, "How Can We Sinners Know," in *The United Methodist Hymnal* (Nashville, Tenn.: United Methodist Publishing House, 1989), no. 372.

15. Fitchett, *Wesley and His Century*, 455.

16. Ibid., 2.

17. Colin W. Williams, *John Wesley's Theology Today* (London: Epworth Press, 1960), 24.

18. Richard P. Heitzenrater, *Wesley and the People Called Methodists* (Nashville, Tenn.: Abingdon Press, 1995), 308.

CHAPTER 11: OLNEY AND JOHN NEWTON

1. Bernard Martin, *An Ancient Mariner: A Biography of John Newton* (London: Epworth Press, 1960), 50.

2. Ibid., 52.

3. Brian H. Edwards, *Through Many Dangers: The Story of John Newton* (Welwyn, Hertfordshire, England: Eurobooks, 1980), 94.

4. Marcus Loane, quoted in introduction to *Letters of John Newton* (London: The Banner of Truth Trust, 1960), 9.

5. Ibid., 10.

6. Ibid., 9.

7. Edwards, *Through Many Dangers*, 95.

8. D. Bruce Hindmarsh, *John Newton and the English Evangelical Tradition* (Grand Rapids, Mich.: William B. Eerdmans Publishing Co., 2001), 258.

9. William Cowper, *Olney Hymns* (Olney, England: The Trustees of The Cowper and Newton Museum, 1979), Book II, Hymn 44, 234.

10. Hindmarsh, *John Newton and the English Evangelical Tradition,* 331.

11. Ian Bradley, ed., *The Penguin Book of Hymns* (London: Penguin Books, 1990), 35. The tune was first published in *Columbian Harmony* (Cincinnati, Oh., 1829) and *The Virginia Harmony* (Winchester, Va., 1831) before being linked to the words of "Amazing Grace."

12. Margaret Cropper, *Life of Evelyn Underhill* (New York: Harper & Brothers, 1958), 165.

13. Edwards, *Through Many Dangers,* 191.

CHAPTER 12: ST. BEUNO'S AND GERARD MANLEY HOPKINS

1. Gerard Manley Hopkins, "Spring," in *Poems and Prose of Gerard Manley Hopkins,* ed. W. H. Gardner (London: Penguin Books, 1985), 28. Hereinafter *Poems.*

2. Hopkins, "Hurrahing in Harvest," in *Poems,* 31.

3. Hopkins, "The Windhover: to Christ Our Lord," in *Poems,* 30.

4. *Poems,* 175.

5. Ibid.

6. Ibid.

7. Robert Bernard Martin, *Gerard Manley Hopkins: A Very Private Life* (New York: G. P. Putnam's Sons, 1991), 174.

8. Ibid., 165.

9. Hopkins, *Poems,* 12 ff. Hopkins submitted *The Wreck of the Deutschland* to *The Month,* a Jesuit literary magazine, which rejected it as incomprehensible. For an account of the effect of this incident on Hopkins, see Norman White, *Hopkins: A Literary Biography* (Oxford: Oxford University Press, 2002), 257–60.

10. St. Beuno's currently offers courses, training programs, and long and short retreats. For information write: St. Beuno's, St. Asaph, Denbighshire, North Wales, LL17 OAS. Tel.: (011-44-1) 745-583-444.

11. Gerard Manley Hopkins, *The Sermons and Devotional Writings of Gerard Manley Hopkins,* ed. Christopher Devlin (London: Oxford University Press, 1959), 225–26.

12. Ibid., 233.

13. Hopkins, *Poems,* 61.

14. Martin, *Gerard Manley Hopkins,* 401.

15. Ibid., 402.

16. Gerard Manley Hopkins, *The Letters of Gerard Manley Hopkins to*

Robert Bridges, ed. Claude Colleer Abbott (London: Oxford University Press, 1955), 76: "The kind people of the sonnet were the Watsons of Shooters Hill, nothing to do with the Elwy."

17. Ignatius of Loyola, *The Spiritual Exercises of Ignatius Loyola,* trans. Anthony Mottola (Garden City, N.Y.: Image Books, 1964), 47.

18. Hopkins, *Sermons and Devotional Writings,* 261.

19. Hopkins, "Editor's Notes," in *Poems,* 237.

20. Hopkins, "The Leaden Echo and the Golden Echo," in *Poems,* 54.

21. Hopkins, "Sonnet No. 34," in *Poems,* 51.

22. White, *Hopkins: A Literary Biography,* 238.

23. Ibid., 243.

24. Hopkins, *Letters,* 40.

25. Gerard Manley Hopkins, *The Journals and Papers of Gerard Manley Hopkins,* ed. Humphry House and Graham Storey (London: Oxford University Press, 1959), 261.

26. Hopkins, *The Wreck of the Deutschland,* in *Poems,* 13.

27. "A Prayer of Self-Dedication," in *The Book of Common Prayer* (New York: The Church Hymnal Corporation, 1979), 832–33.

28. Ignatius, *Spiritual Exercises,* 38.

CHAPTER 13: PLESHEY AND EVELYN UNDERHILL

1. C. S. Lewis, *Surprised by Joy: The Shape of My Early Life* (London: FontanaBooks, 1959), 14.

2. Evelyn Underhill, *The Mystics of the Church* (London: James Clarke & Co., 1925; first U.S. edition, Harrisburg, Pa.: Morehouse Publishing, 1975).

3. Evelyn Underhill, *Evelyn Underhill: Modern Guide to the Ancient Quest for the Holy,* ed. Dana Greene (Albany, N.Y.: State University of New York Press, 1988), 150.

4. Ibid., 137.

5. Ibid., 156.

6. Christopher Armstrong, *Evelyn Underhill: An Introduction to Her Life and Writings* (London: Mowbray, 1975), 1.

7. See Fay Campbell, "Evelyn Underhill: Conversion at Pleshey," *The Living Church* (1 March 1987), 11–13.

8. Margaret Cropper, *The Life of Evelyn Underhill: An Intimate Portrait of the Groundbreaking Author of Mysticism* (Woodstock, Vt.: Skylight Paths Publishing, 2003), 24.

9. Dana Greene, ed., *Evelyn Underhill: Modern Guide,* 138.

10. Cropper, *The Life of Evelyn Underhill ,* 67.

11. Ibid., 87–88.

12. Ibid., 89.

13. Evelyn Underhill, *The Letters of Evelyn Underhill,* ed. Charles Williams (London: Longmans, Green and Co., 1943), 150.

14. T. S. Eliot, cited in Helen Gardner, *The Composition of Four Quartets* (London: Faber and Faber, 1978), 70.

15. Evelyn Underhill, *Light of Christ* (London: Longmans, Green and Co., 1944), 102.

16. Lucy Menzies, "Memoir," in *Light of Christ,* 12–13.

17. Evelyn Underhill, from an article in the *Church Times,* March 1933, quoted in *Pleshey: The Village and Retreat House* by Margaret Avery (Bishop's Stortford, England: Ellis & Phillips, 1981), 41–42.

18. Underhill, *Light of Christ,* 34.

19. Underhill, "Possibilities of Prayer," in Dana Greene, ed., *Evelyn Underhill,* 149.

20. Evelyn Underhill, *Spiritual Life* (London: Mowbray, 1984), 93.

CHAPTER 14: COVENTRY CATHEDRAL

1. R. T. Howard quoted in Charles Wilkinson, *Spirit of Britain: A Pilgrimage of Faith and Pride* (Ancaster, Ontario: Pilgrim Paperbacks,1987), 85.

2. Basil Spence, *Phoenix at Coventry: The Building of a Cathedral* (London: Geoffrey Bles, 1962), 17.

3. Ibid., 20.

4. Ibid., 106.

5. Wilfred Owen, "Insensibility," in *The Penguin Book of First World War Poetry* (Harmondsworth, Middlesex, England: Penguin Books, 1981), 191.

6. Wilkinson, *Spirit of Britain,* 86.

7. Spence, *Phoenix at Coventry,* vii.

8. Paul Oestreicher, *The Double Cross* (Wilton, Conn.: Morehouse-Barlow, 1986), 1; telephone interviews 21 July 2003 and 21 July 1998.

9. C. S. Lewis, "On Forgiveness," in *Fern-seed and Elephants: And Other Essays on Christianity* (Glasgow: Fount Paperbacks, 1977), 40.

10. Johann Christoph Arnold, *The Lost Art of Forgiving: Stories of Healing from the Cancer of Bitterness* (Farmington, Pa: Plough Publishing House, 1998), 122.

11. C. S. Lewis, "On Forgiveness," *Fern-seed and Elephants,* 39.

12. Alan Paton quoted in Arnold, *The Lost Art of Forgiving,* xii.

13. Oestreicher, *The Double Cross,* 45; telephone interviews 21 July 2003 and 21 July 1998.

14. Corrie ten Boom, *The Hiding Place* (New York: Bantam Books, 1974), 238.

15. Kyle A. Pasewark, "Remembering to Forget: A Politics of Forgiveness," *Christian Century* (5–12 July 1995), 684.

CHAPTER 15: OXFORD AND C. S. LEWIS

1. C. S. Lewis, *The Silver Chair* (New York: The Macmillan Company, 1953), 8.

2. Humphrey Carpenter, *The Inklings: C. S. Lewis, J. R.. R.. Tolkien, Charles Williams, and Their Friends* (Boston: Houghton Mifflin Company, 1979), 43.

3. C. S. Lewis, *Surprised by Joy: The Shape of My Early Life* (New York: Harcourt, Brace and Company, 1956), 17.

4. J. R. R. Tolkien, "On Fairy-Stories," in *Essays Presented to Charles Williams* (Grand Rapids, Mich.: William B. Eerdmans Publishing Co., 1966), 81.

5. Lewis, *Surprised by Joy,* 16.

6. Ibid., 7.

7. Ibid., 6.

8. Ibid., 19.

9. C. S. Lewis, "The Weight of Glory," in *The Weight of Glory and Other Addresses* (Grand Rapids, Mich: William B. Eerdmans Publishing Co., 1965), 12.

10. C. S. Lewis, *The Pilgrim's Regress: An Allegorical Apology for Christianity Reason and Romanticism* (Grand Rapids, Mich.: William B. Eerdmans Publishing Co., 1958), 148.

11. C. S. Lewis, *Mere Christianity* (New York: Macmillan Publishing Co., 1960),120.

12. C. S. Lewis, *The Weight of Glory and Other Addresses,* 12.

13. Lewis to Dom Bede Griffiths, 5 November 1959, *Letters of C. S. Lewis,* ed. W. H. Lewis (New York: Harcourt, Brace & World, 1966), 289.

14. *Till We Have Faces: A Myth Retold* (Grand Rapids, Mich: William B. Eerdmans Publishing Co., 1966), 75.

15. C. S. Lewis, *The Lion, the Witch and the Wardrobe* (Harmondsworth, Middlesex, England: Penguin Books, 1959), 164.

16. The Lewis brothers also shared the house with Mrs. Janie Moore, the mother of a friend of C. S. Lewis who died in World War I. For an account of this remarkable relationship, see George Sayer, *Jack: C. S. Lewis and His Times* (San Francisco: Harper & Row, 1988).

17. C. S. Lewis, *Surprised by Joy*, 224–25.

18. Ibid., 227–28.

19. C. S. Lewis to Warren H. Lewis, 22 November 1931, unpublished letter cited in Sayer, *Jack*, 143.

20. Lewis, *Surprised by Joy*, 181.

21. Lewis, *The Weight of Glory and Other Addresses*, 12–13.

22. Lewis, *The Silver Chair*, 186–87.

23. Ibid., 192.

CHAPTER 16: LITTLE GIDDING AND NICHOLAS FERRAR & T. S. ELIOT

1. Lyndall Gordon, *T. S. Eliot: An Imperfect Life* (New York: W. W. Norton, 2000), 370.

2. See Helen Gardner, *The Art of T. S. Eliot* (London: The Cresset Press, 1949),183–84.

3. Ronald Schuchard, "If I think, again, of this place': Eliot, Herbert, and the Way to 'Little Gidding,'" *Words in Time: New Essays on Eliot's* Four Quartets, ed. Edward Lobb (London: Athlone Press, 1993), 52.

4. See Helen Gardner, *The Composition of Four Quartets* (London: Faber and Faber, 1978), 157.

5. T. S. Eliot, "Little Gidding," *Four Quartets,* in *The Complete Poems and Plays 1909–1950* (New York: Harcourt Brace Jovanovich, 1980), 139.

6. Ibid., 144.

7. Ibid., 139.

8. *The Little Gidding Prayer Book* (London: SPCK, 1986), 1.

9. Robert Van de Weyer, *Little Gidding: Story and Guide* (London: Lamp Press, 1989), 50.

10. Robert Van de Weyer, *The Little Gidding Way: Christian Community for Ordinary People* (London: Darton Longman & Todd, 1988), 86.

11. Brigid E. Herman, *Creative Prayer,* ed. Hal M. Helms (Brewster, Mass.: Paraclete Press, 1998), 25.

12. Ibid.

13. Van de Weyer, *The Little Gidding Way*, 7–8.

14. T. S. Eliot, "East Coker," *Four Quartets,* in *The Complete Poems and Plays,* 128.

15. Eliot, "Little Gidding," in *The Complete Poems and Plays*, 139.

16. See Gardner, *The Composition of Four Quartets*, 163.

17. Eliot, "Little Gidding," in *The Complete Poems and Plays,* 139.

18. A. L. Maycock, *Nicholas Ferrar of Little Gidding* (London: Society for Promoting Christian Knowledge, 1938), 126.

19. Eliot, "Little Gidding," in *The Complete Poems and Plays,* 145.

20. Julian of Norwich, *Julian of Norwich: Showings,* trans. Edmund Colledge and James Walsh, Classics of Western Spirituality (New York: Paulist Press, 1978), 225. See also Eliot, *The Complete Poems and Plays,* 145.

Publishing Acknowledgments

Portions of this book have appeared as titled in the following publications:

Douglas, David. "Ninian's Whithorn: A Time-and-Place Pilgrimage," *Review for Religious* 56, no. 5 (September–October 1997): 525–32.

Douglas, Deborah Smith. "'Stand Fast': Saint Columba and the Isle of Iona," *Weavings* 13, no. 4 (July/August 1998): 6–14.

Douglas, David. "England's Holy Island (Lindisfarne)," *Catholic Digest* (July 1998): 18–29.

Douglas, Deborah Smith. "Tiny Island of Prayer: St. Margaret's Chapel," *Living Church* 215, no. 20 (16 November 1997): 16.

Douglas, David. "The Growing Company of Martyrs: Reflections from Canterbury Cathedral's East Chapel," *Touchstone* 13, no. 10 (December 2000): 16–19.

Douglas, Deborah Smith. "Julian of Norwich: 'God at the Centre of Everything,'" *Weavings* 13, no. 1 (January/February 1998): 6–15.

Douglas, Deborah Smith. "George Herbert at Bemerton: 'Thy Power and Love, My Love and Trust,'" *Weavings* 14, no. 3 (May/June 1999), 14–25.

Douglas, Deborah Smith. "Standing Fast on the Pilgrim Way: Margaret Clitherow and Mary Ward," *Weavings* 15, no. 6 (November/December 2000): 25–32.

Douglas, David. "In Search of Pendle Hill and George Fox," *Friends Journal,* no. 6 (June 1999): 6–8.

Douglas, David. "An American Investigates [Wesley's Aldersgate Experience]," *Epworth Review* 26 (January 1999): 60–65.

Douglas, David. "Amazing Grace: A Journey in Time and Faith (Olney & John Newton)," *The Hymn* 49, no. 3 (July 1998): 9–12, copyright The Hymn Society. Used by permission.

Douglas, Deborah Smith. "Gerard Manley Hopkins at St. Beunos: 'Steady as a Water in a Well,'" *Christianity and the Arts* 7, no. 2 (Spring 2000), 32–37.

Douglas, Deborah Smith. "Evelyn Underhill at Pleshey," *Weavings* 14, no. 1 (January/February 1999): 15–25.

Douglas, David. "Coventry Cathedral's Message of Forgiveness," *Review for Religious* 58, no. 6 (November–December 1999): 643–48.

Douglas, Deborah Smith. "C. S. Lewis and Our Longing for Home: The Deepest Thirst within Us," *Weavings* 15, no. 4 (July/August 2000): 6–17.

The publisher gratefully acknowledges permission to reprint the following copyrighted material:

Excerpt from "Burnt Norton" in *Four Quartets* by T. S. Eliot. Copyright 1936 by Harcourt, Inc. and renewed 1964 by T. S. Eliot. Reprinted by permission of the publisher and Faber & Faber, Ltd.

Excerpts from "East Coker" in *Four Quartets*. Copyright 1940 by T. S. Eliot and renewed 1968 by Esme Valerie Eliot. Reprinted by permission of Harcourt, Inc. and Faber & Faber, Ltd.

Excerpts from *GEORGE HERBERT: The Country Parson, The Temple,* edited, with an introduction by John N. Wall Jr., preface by A. M. Allchin, from the Classics of Western Spirituality, Copyright © 1981 by Paulist Press, Inc., New York/Mahwah, N.J. Used with permission of Paulist Press. www.paulist-press.com

Excerpts from "Little Gidding" in *Four Quartets*. Copyright 1942 by T. S. Eliot and renewed 1970 by Esme Valerie Eliot. Reprinted by permission of the publisher and Faber & Faber, Ltd.

Index

Museum of Methodism, 115, 116, 215
Mush, John, 98
Muslims, 68
"My Life Is Hid in Him That Is My Treasure"
    (Herbert), 88–89
mysticism, 144–47, 189
Mystics of the Church, The (Underhill),
    144, 145

N

Native Americans, 112
nature, 135–36, 172
Nazis, 65, 68, 155–56
needlepoint, 85, 144, 145
"New Britain," 126
New Mexico, 14, 182
Newton, John, 113, 121–28, 188, 217–18,
    227
    stained-glass window of, 124
Newton, Mary, 124
Nicholas Ferrar of Little Gidding (Maycock),
    190
Ninian, Saint, 194–95
    cave/monastery of, 19–26, 30
    stained-glass window of, 53
Norman Conquest, 54
Northern Ireland, 69, 161
Northumberland, England, 41
Norwich, England, 14, 73–81, 204–6
Norwich Cathedral, 80, 205
nostalgia, 173

O

"O Clap Your Hands" (Williams), 63
"O! for a Closer Walk with God" (Cowper),
    125
"O for a Thousand Tongues to Sing"
    (Wesley), 117
Oestreicher, Paul, 161–62, 164, 165
Olney, 14, 16, 121–28, 188, 217–18, 227
Olney Hymns (Newton and Cowper), 16,
    121, 125, 217, 227
Operation Moonlight Sonata, 155
Oran's Chapel, 33
Owen, Wilfred, 160
Oxford, England, 14, 169–79, 224–25
Oxford Tower, 70

P

paganism, 21
parable of the unforgiving servant, 163–64
Paradise, 172
Pasewark, Kyle, 165
Passion, the, 76–77
Paterson, John L., 33
Paton, Alan, 164
Paul, apostle, 44, 70, 104, 114, 118
    "Be kind to one another," 165
    giant of Christian prayer, 144
    Damascus road experience, 111, 112, 113
Pelagianism, 126
pelicans, 80
Pendle Hill, 101–8, 213–14
Penguin Book of Hymns, The (Bradley), 126
Penn, William, 106
Perry, Richard, 45
Phantases (MacDonald), 177
Phoenix at Coventry (Spence), 158–59
Picts, 15, 21
Pilgrim's Progress, The (Bunyan), 17, 125, 188,
    218, 227
Piper, John, 159
Places in the Heart, 186
Pleshey, 143–52, 221–22
Poet's Corner, 134
prayer, 24, 36, 144–48, 151
    common, 161
    contemplative, 145, 206
    Coventry Litany of Reconciliation, 165, 223
    forgiveness and, 156–57, 163, 165–66
    life of, 145, 146
    Little Gidding, 182, 184, 186, 188, 190
    Lord's Prayer, 163, 189
    Morning and Evening, 86
    unitive, 144–45
    "where prayer has been valid," 25, 226
priests, 94–99
Princes Street Gardens, 58–59
Protestant-Catholic strife, 69, 94–99
Psalm
    18:2, 61
    61:2–3, 34

Q

Quakers, 17, 101–8, 116, 185, 213–14
Queen Elizabeth Gardens, 207

About the Authors

DEBORAH SMITH DOUGLAS grew up in Kansas and received degrees from Duke University in English literature and the University of Kansas in law. Trained in spiritual direction, she has led retreats in the United States and Britain. Her articles on prayer have been published in numerous magazines, and her book *The Praying Life: Finding God in All Things* was published by Morehouse in 2003.

DAVID DOUGLAS, born in Washington, D.C., received degrees from the College of Wooster in religious studies and the University of Colorado in law. He has written extensively for environmental and religious magazines and published *Wilderness Sojourn: Notes in the Desert Silence* (Harper, 1987). He heads the nonprofit WATERLINES, which works to provide safe drinking water to rural communities in developing countries.

Married since 1978, Deborah and David have two daughters, Katie and Emily. While researching and writing this book, they spent two years in St. Andrews, Scotland. Though both have roots deep in the Presbyterian Church, Deborah is now an Episcopalian and a Benedictine oblate, and David worships at Protestant and Catholic churches. Their writing about places and people associated with Christianity in Britain has appeared in *Weavings, Review for Religious, Epworth Review, Catholic Digest, Living Church, The Hymn, Christianity and the Arts, Touchstone,* and *Friends Journal.* They live in Santa Fe, New Mexico, and return frequently to the United Kingdom.

About the Photographer

Joan Myers, the photographer whose images appear in this book, has had her work exhibited internationally. Her images are represented in the collections of many major institutions and individuals, including the Museum of Modern Art, the Amon Carter Museum, the Bibliotèque Nationale, and the National Gallery of Art, Smithsonian Institution. She is best known for photographing the interaction between people and landscapes. Her last book, *Salt Dreams: Land and Water in Low-Down California,* documents her ten-year study of the environmental issues facing the Salton Sea in southern California. Most recently, she received a National Science Foundation Artists and Writers grant to photograph in Antarctica.

Myers's photographs for *Pilgrims in the Kingdom* reflect her interest in history visible in the landscape. "Inevitably, the sites in this book became part of a personal journey of discovery. For me, as for many pilgrims before me, that journey became more important than the destination, the life changes as important as the photographs that were taken," she says.

Educated at Stanford, Myers currently lives and works in Santa Fe, New Mexico. For further information, see the photographer's Web site at www.joanmyers.com.